"Krauss offers the roadmap we need to get kids ready for a rapidly changing and challenging world. Her call for every adult and educator to become a currency-builder is one we should take seriously. This is a must-read."

Arne Duncan, managing partner of Emerson Collective and former US Secretary of Education

"Smart and insightful! Stephanie Malia Krauss makes a compelling case for the new currencies kids need to thrive in our rapidly changing world."

Cal Newport, *New York Times* bestselling author of *Digital Minimalism* and *Deep Work*

"Krauss is an educator who knows that learning is not to be confused with schooling. She demonstrates brilliantly that complex ideas can be communicated clearly, and with some wit. Drawing on her own professional and personal experience, she shows in this lively book that academic qualifications are necessary, but far from sufficient. Being ready to 'make it' today requires skills and connections acquired far from the classroom. Inequalities in the first two decades of life echo through working lives; 'making it' has become a near-certainty for children born to affluent, educated, healthy parents but an ever-steeper challenge for those born to poor parents, and those facing the obstacles of anti-Black racism. Krauss wants making it to be a right, rather than a privilege. The hope animating this book is that we can find 'beauty in the brokenness' of our current moment. Timely, wise, and inspiring."

Richard V. Reeves, Senior Fellow at Brookings Institution, and Author of *Dream Hoarders*

"With her trademark blend of liveliness and concrete, realistic advice, Stephanie Malia Krauss writes about what the future holds for today's kids – and what youth workers, families and allies can do to help prepare them. Easy to read, and with ideas you will return to."

Leslie Lapides, senior editor, *Youth Today*

"What will it take for children growing up today to 'make it' in a society that is changing so rapidly? Stephanie Malia Krauss's magnificent book explores this important question and provides creative pathways to ensure a better future for our kids."

John Bridgeland, CEO of Civic and former director of the White House Domestic Policy Council

"In *Making It*, Krauss powerfully equips parents, educators and policymakers to be currency-builders for young people facing tomorrow's ever-changing world. Kids need competencies, connections, credentials, and cash – whole-life solutions preparing them for long, livable lives. Krauss writes in a way that is crisp, engaging, and inspiring."

Anne Holton, professor of Education Policy at George Mason University and former Virginia Secretary of Education

"This eye-opening and inspirational book shares a treasure trove of creative perspectives that will change the ways we think about quality education. It should be required reading for educators, youth workers, parents, child advocates, and policymakers who want to understand today's kids and implement innovative, practical strategies that prepare all young people to achieve well-being and success in tomorrow's world."

Roger Weissberg, PhD, Distinguished Professor Emeritus of Psychology at University of Illinois at Chicago and chief knowledge officer for Collaborative for Academic, Social, and Emotional Learning (CASEL)

"*Making It* is essential reading for anyone who is parenting and supporting young people in 2020 and beyond."

Rhonda Broussard, CEO of Beloved Community

"It's clear the old 'checklist for adulthood' doesn't work. Krauss builds a credible case for competencies, credentials, connections, and cash as the new currencies of the innovation economy. Among prescriptions of what learners should know and be able to do, *Making It* is the first book that takes a whole person approach and deals credibly with the new economic realities and outlines strategies 'where young people learn into currency-rich environments.' The concluding chapter on Becoming a Currency Builder is a must-read for parents, teachers, youth-developers, and civic leaders – it's a formula for building just, inclusive, and caring communities."

Tom Vander Ark, CEO of Getting Smart

"Anyone who aims to improve the ecosystems of children and youth will not only benefit from but will also enjoy reading *Making It*. Mayors, superintendents, healthcare providers, out-of-school time providers, community-based organizations, and many other who touch the lives of children will gain an important framing of what it takes for our kids to 'make it' in a rapidly evolving world. Thank you, Stephanie, for writing this readable and accessible book that will help us all serve kids better!"

Bridget Rodriguez, managing director of EdRedesign at the Harvard Graduate School of Education

"In her new book *Making It*, Stephanie Malia Krauss delivers a wake-up call about the need to align the core of American education with the everchanging demands of the workplace. She lays out a compelling vision of the currencies that will be essential to adults in coming decades and argues persuasively for a wholesale reimagination of how we educate all students – from toddlers through adults seeking to upgrade skills. For a roadmap to a better future, dive into this book!"

Ted Dintersmith, founder of *The What School Could Be* Foundation

"*Making It* is the book that Stephanie Malia Krauss was destined to write. With each page, she lays out a logical and comprehensive roadmap of what all of us need to do to ensure that our children enter a world for which not only they are prepared academically, but a world that reflects improved values, justice and human-centered priorities. Knowing Stephanie and having had the distinct pleasure of working alongside of her in creating better opportunities for Virginia's children, this book does what she does so very well – it creates a vision of what could be and designs a process to actually make it happen. We owe it to our children, especially those underserved, to do all in our power to deliver to them a future that is full of promise, wonder and curiosity. *Making It* does just that. From my vantage point, there is no more time to waste. This book will inspire you to action. It did me."

Steve Constantino, internationally recognized speaker on family and community engagement; executive professor for the School of Education at William and Mary; author of *Engage Every Family: Five Simple Principles;* and former chief academic officer and acting state superintendent in Virginia

"A vision for today's kids, a vision made actionable through science, case examples, personal stories, and inspiration. This is what Stephanie Malia Krauss has achieved in *Making It*. If you care about humanity, then *Making It* is for you – whether you are a parent, policymaker, voter, educator, or social worker. Our collective future depends on enacting the vision advanced in this book."

Amanda Moore McBride, Morris Endowed Dean and professor of the Graduate School of Social Work at the University of Denver

"*Making It* is an important source for understanding the multiple challenges facing today's children and youth, and how successfully to assure their learning and development. In our rapidly changing world, it provides a framework for building currencies that provide pathways to success of all children in school and life."

Mark Ginsberg, provost and executive vice president of George Mason University, and the former dean of the College of Education and Human Development at George Mason University

"In a world with so much uncertainty, *Making It* makes loads of sense. Stephanie's honest and just approach to currency-building changes the calculus of an unfair system to a whole-life approach about well-being developed overtime and not by time."

Elliot Washor, co-founder and director of Big Picture Learning

"We know it's not just about academic achievement, but what else do young people need to make it in today's complicated world? Stephanie Malia Krauss carefully and clearly lays it out: an interwoven set of competencies, network of connections, recognized credentials, and necessary financial resources. Unarguably, these 'currencies' are harder to come by for Black, brown, and indigenous young people, and others whose experiences and identities our white-centered systems were designed to disadvantage. If you believe every kid is entitled to make it, this book will challenge you to become a 'currency-builder' – and show you how to do it."

Kathleen Traphagen, lead facilitator of *Grantmakers for Thriving Youth* and *Grantmakers for Education's Out-of-School Time Impact Group*

"*Making It* is a uniquely powerful book, offering a clear, concrete roadmap for parents and educators who want to equip our children to lead fundamentally meaningful lives amidst the overwhelming pace of economic, technological, and social change. As 2020 draws to a close, Stephanie's compelling Life Currencies framework could not be more timely as we focus attention, in earnest, on remodeling our institutions for a more hopeful and just future."

Cyrus E. Driver, senior director, Partnership for the Future of Learning

"*Making It* is a must-read for anyone trying to navigate the complexities of education in the 21st century. The book weaves together research on the future of work and the future of learning with decades of research on human development and social mobility, not to mention Krauss's firsthand experiences in policy and practice. The result? *Making It* paints a detailed picture of what students will need for a future of thriving."

Julia Freeland Fisher, director of Education Research at the Clayton Christensen Institute and author of *Who You Know: Unlocking Innovations that Expand Students' Networks*

"*Making It* positions today's students and families importantly as *consumers* in the education market, who must now make sense of the more than 700,000 credentials out there and adopt new mindsets about what it means to prepare for an increasingly uncertain world of work ahead."

Michelle R. Weise, author of *Long Life Learning: Preparing for Jobs that Don't Even Exist Yet*

"Make this book your required reading for 2021. In *Making It*, author Stephanie Malia Krauss labels the state of today's volatile and unpredictable times as 'the overwhelm.' Stephanie frames this century's grand American challenge as ensuring young people – all of them, especially children of color or those living in impoverished homes – gain what they need to thrive, not just survive, as adults. She lays out a reimagined educational path delineated by social and economic justice to enable all young people to navigate toward currency-driven success in life as they acquire competencies, cash, connections, and credentials. *Making it* defines a social contract to educate *all* learners well – a contract that's long overdue."

Pamela Moran, executive director of the Virginia School Consortium for Learning and co-author of *Timeless Learning*

"If you fear the current education system is outdated, *Making It* is a must-read to deliberately create mind space to reimagine what is possible. It offers honest insights about future trends and disruptions, including questioning the value of current qualifications like the high school diploma toward meaningful credentials. It asks for revamping graduation requirements and rethinking meaningful credentials on what a valuable high-quality diploma might look like. This requires recognizing, undoing, and correcting the persistent inequities that harm kids in today's traditional education system focused on ranking and sorting kids, as well as stopping damaging privilege hoarding. It challenges adults to do the important work of grappling with uncertainties and turning to science on youth development to provide new opportunities through educational and economic pathways."

Susan Patrick, CEO of Aurora Institute

"There are deep chasms in the opportunities young people have to accrue the currencies Krauss so clearly describes in *Making It*. Her book brings the study of youth development into current times. My blended family of three adolescent boys will benefit from me having read this, and my advocacy with state and local policymakers across this country will also surely benefit. This should be required reading for anyone shaping public policy beyond 2020."

Elizabeth Gaines, founder and director of Children's Funding Project

Making It

Making It

What Today's Kids Need for Tomorrow's World

Stephanie Malia Krauss

JB JOSSEY-BASS™
A Wiley Brand

A Wiley Brand
111 River Street, Hoboken NJ 07030
www.josseybass.com

Jossey-Bass books and products are available through most bookstores. To contact Jossey-Bass directly call our Customer Care Department within the US at 800-956-7739, outside the US at 317-572-3986, or fax 317-572-4002.

Wiley also publishes its books in a variety of electronic formats and by print-on-demand. Some material included with standard print versions of this book may not be included in e-books or in print-on-demand. For more information about Wiley products, visit www.wiley.com.

Library of Congress Cataloging-in-Publication Data
Names: Krauss, Stephanie Malia, 1985- author.
Title: Making it : what today's kids need for tomorrow's world / Stephanie Malia Krauss.
Description: Hoboken, NJ : Jossey-Bass, [2021]
Identifiers: LCCN 2020047586 (print) | LCCN 2020047587 (ebook) | ISBN 9781119577034 (cloth) | ISBN 9781119577010 (adobe pdf) | ISBN 9781119577072 (epub)
Subjects: LCSH: Life skills—Study and teaching (Secondary) | School-to-work transition. | Career education. | Education—Aims and objectives.
Classification: LCC LC1037 .K73 2021 (print) | LCC LC1037 (ebook) | DDC 370.113—dc23
LC record available at https://lccn.loc.gov/2020047586
LC ebook record available at https://lccn.loc.gov/2020047587

COVER ART: © TANYA ST / ISTOCKPHOTO
COVER DESIGN: PAUL MCCARTHY

Printed in the United States of America
SKY10024166_011821

To the currency-builders who helped me make it, especially Mrs. Lewis and Jim.

To my kids—Justice, Harrison, Chloe, and Brian—may you have everything you need to thrive and make it in tomorrow's world.

To my husband, Evan. I am so glad you are the person I get to experience adulthood with. I love you very much.

CONTENTS

■ ■ ■

■ ■ ■

PREFACE

All authors want to write an evergreen book, and I am no exception. In *Making It*, I wanted to present enduring ideas with as much relevance for today's kids as tomorrow's. And writing wrapped up just as COVID-19 pummeled the planet into the worst public health and economic crises we have seen in our lifetimes; my final edits were made soon after the high-profile anti-Black murders of George Floyd, Breonna Taylor, and Ahmaud Arbery—along with innumerable other acts of racial profiling and violence. These led to unrest and uprisings as well as a growing number of acknowledgments of racism by many in the white community. Many made a first-time commitment to work toward being antiracist.

The year 2020 magnifies what happens when a centuries-old pandemic—America's brand of racism and anti-Blackness—collides with an altogether new pandemic, COVID-19.

As I write this, we are in the midst of pandemic schooling, and no public health official, politician, pediatrician, or principal really knows what will happen. COVID-19 cases continue to rise, prompting fear from many and denial from others. As a mother of school-aged children, I am forced to accept that this is the world and time my children will grow up in.

In the following pages, you'll find stories of what it takes and the struggles that many children face as they try to make it in America. And in that struggle, I cannot help but see my own privilege and my children's good fortune. I am able to make choices for them right now that are only possible because of our whiteness and wealth. I can choose to have them learning at home with digital supports at our fingertips. I can take them on trips, wherever and whenever we want, without fear, because we are white. Yet, I wrestle with the choices I am making and how they might contribute to worsening segregation and the deep racial and class divides that exist in our nation.

This book reflects these tensions, because it tackles what any young person in America needs to make it into and through adulthood. I wrote it because I have heard from young people, educators, and parents who want a better roadmap to navigate the world as it is, in a country that is still unfair and unjust—a country with an origin story of European settlers taking land that belonged to others, and declaring it their own.

To really be about the business of helping young people make it in the world, we must operate on two planes: the one we are living in and the one we are building. We must help young people get what they need to survive in a place that does not live up to its promise of equal opportunity for all. This requires—among other things—a genuine commitment to antiracism, which takes constant reflection and action, and a willingness to be wrong and make it right. It also requires that those of us who are white take a posture of listening and learning, something I continue to try to get better at.

Today's kids need adults who will stand up and call out bigotry and oppressive action toward young people of color, those who are disabled, the LGBTQIA community, and other marginalized groups. We must seek to understand who is hardest hit and most held back, figuring out what more they need to make it. But doing this alone is not sufficient. We must also work with those young people to co-create new rules of living and being, rooted in equity and justice. These young people are already taking the lead, and they need adults to help them carry out their visions for the future. This is individual and collective work, and it is at once introspective, expressive, and constructive.

In this year of immense loss and struggle, I think about our children and about how this reality is all they know. While there is so much we don't have control over, there is so much we do. We can find beauty in the brokenness, because there is still hope and space to reimagine.

If we get this right, then maybe one day our children can write the book *Made It*—a history book about how they had what they needed—not just to get by, but to build a better tomorrow.

Stephanie Malia Krauss
November 2020

FOREWORD BY
KAREN PITTMAN

Stephanie Krauss is a force of nature. A colleague introduced Stephanie to me at a conference I was keynoting in St. Louis some years ago. It took only a few minutes for me to experience the depth of her passion and intellect. It took less than an hour for me to commit to helping her figure out how to bring the incredible lessons she had learned—in life and by running a charter school for undercredited, overage students—to the national stage. That commitment resulted in a quickly negotiated fellowship with the Forum that served as the springboard for friendship and colleagueship that gets richer with every opportunity we tackle together—formal or informal.

Our first colleagueship project remains, by far, the most ambitious. It started with an audacious challenge: create a universal list of competencies youth need to succeed that speaks clearly to young people, resonates with leaders across multiple systems (from education to juvenile justice), and is grounded in everything we know about learning and development. This was something the Forum staff and I had dreamed of for years, but never tackled. An hour into her first staff meeting, however, we knew Stephanie was up to the task.

Stephanie shared with our team that in an effort to make high school graduation requirements relevant and reachable for students—many of whom were, on traditional measures, four or more years behind—Stephanie and her staff had broken down the Missouri graduation requirements into 21 accessible competencies that students needed to master before their 21st birthdays. They called it "21 by 21." Brilliant idea. Accessible results. It was an unbalanced list, however, because too many competencies focused on specific academic skills. When asked about the imbalance, Stephanie answered that she had to start with the academic skills to meet accountability requirements. She squeezed broader life skills in where she could.

Ready by Design: The Science (and Art) of Youth Readiness was the down payment on a gift we hoped to deliver to practitioners and administrators who work with young people in all of the settings where learning and development can, should, and usually does happen. The gift stayed in layaway for lack of funding. But the ideas, and our passion for making them accessible across fields and systems, remained. Our strategy, even as we went our separate ways, has been to encourage decision-makers to put young people and their drive to beat the odds at the center of every discussion and decision. Our secret goal, of course, was to find a way to complete the down payment and deliver the gift.

Stephanie has delivered. And the gift is needed now more than ever. 2020 will go down as the year in which almost every assumption about why some young people "make it" and others don't is tested; about the relative importance of the assets families, schools, community organizations and the larger community, as well as social, physical, and economic contexts play in a young person's success; and, about the underlying reasons behind the huge disparities in assets. 2020 will go down as the year in which educators—in classrooms, clubhouses, courthouses, camps, and community centers—openly acknowledge that the tools and plans they have are not sufficient for the massive design-build job at hand.

This book starts with the question, "What does it take to ensure young people are ready?" This is the right place to start. This is not because we don't need to improve our schools (the starting place for many books). It is because schools are a means to an end, and when the end is defined narrowly as an academic credential, the opportunity to explore all of the pathways to success and understand all of the barriers is truncated. COVID has moved us into what will likely be a new wave of school reimagining efforts.

This book, and others like it, can help those charged with directly supporting young people's development with the confidence and narratives they need to actively balance the requirements of the education system—which focuses on academic competence and academic credentials—with a broader awareness of the whole ecosystem young people are in, forging connections and building broader competencies, which is hampered or buoyed by their ability to access cash and credit.

Making It is not a review of curricula or exemplary programs. It is a big-picture overview of the forces that influence young people's ability to focus, learn, grow, and succeed. In the following pages, Stephanie masterfully:

- Breaks down the science of how learning and development happen—giving accessible, useful references and examples not only of how our minds process and make meaning, but of how stress and information overload interfere with learning, how demands and opportunities that youth face will make it even harder for them to manage their learning journeys (formal and informal), and what adults—from families to educators—can do to protect and guide.
- Makes sense out of what has often become a cacophony of acronyms and skill lists, building directly on the work we started in *Ready by Design*. Even if you consider yourself SEL-literate, this section is worth a careful read.
- Makes it clear that credentials and competencies are different and that neither are sufficient to ensure success.
- Gives us five clear, important things we can do to be currency-builders that link directly to the research and translate easily into action.

When we hit the road to popularize the ideas in *Ready by Design*, we coined the phrase "readiness is a right." I had this phrase in mind as I read the manuscript. Readiness is defined as both the capacity and the motivation to tackle challenges and opportunities that come your way.

As we think about what it takes to make readiness a right, we have to reflect on the fact that many of this country's young people are engaged in a much more basic fight to make humanity a right. Black Lives Matter does matter.

This book lays out a powerful argument for why we need to broaden our understanding of what it takes to "make it" as a young person today, and what it will take for the next generation, who could live to be 100. It offers stark examples of the privileges that come with wealth in this country and, in contrast, the challenges that poverty compounds. It acknowledges but does not lead with the fact that there are Black and brown young people in this country, and particularly Black young men, who are struggling and suffering and standing together because their right to live free in their communities is challenged every day.

Stephanie's "light touch" approach is intentional, and the ideas in this book are meant to be a starting place. I know because I asked. The fact that I contributed this foreword shows that Stephanie understands and continues to grapple with these realities, as reflected in her preface.

Competencies, credentials, connections, and cash are the currencies needed to make it in this country. They are all you need if you are white. If you are Black, indigenous, or a person of color, however, making the commitment to build these currencies has to be coupled with a critical analysis of why they have been denied historically, and why the systems charged with your success are still operating under rules that were designed for your failure.

As a Black woman with children and grandchildren, I will call out the need to acknowledge a fifth quality to accompany the currencies, one that enables young people of color to not only make it but to thrive: collective identity. I look forward to hearing more about this in Stephanie's next book.

Karen J. Pittman
Co-Founder, President & CEO
The Forum for Youth Investment

FOREWORD BY
MARIA FLYNN

How do we connect current and future workers to high-paying, in-demand jobs? I've devoted my professional life to answering that question. In truth, it's always been more than a career to me.

Stephanie and I are both "Jersey Girls." I grew up outside of Trenton, New Jersey, immersed in issues of workforce development. My father was a leader at the New Jersey Department of Labor, and my mother was the office manager at our local career and technical education high school. Discussions of the intersection of school and work—from state policy considerations to the plight of students struggling to find their way—were constants at our dinner table.

Now, decades later, Stephanie and I both have the privilege of being moms. She has two boys, and I have two girls. Like all moms, I want my daughters to have the tools they need to thrive in the workforce. Today, that's not a simple task. The formula I was taught—go to college, get a job, advance my career, and eventually (hopefully!) retire—is outdated. It won't work for my daughters—or Stephanie's sons. Nor will it work for their peers. The world today, marked by constant technological innovation, moves too quickly. And for too many individuals across the country currently in the labor force, that "traditional" formula already isn't working. This is particularly true for Black and brown Americans, *one in five of whom is living in poverty* at the time of this writing.

Our education and workforce systems are failing these individuals from a young age, preventing them from reaching their potentials and succeeding in the workforce. In a society in which postsecondary degrees are directly correlated with higher earnings, Black students receive only 14 percent of all associate's degrees and just 11 percent of all bachelor's degrees conferred today.[1] This not only reflects the deep inequities and unjust outcomes that pervade the world of education and work, but it reveals a true loss to society on a broader scale—think of all the talent and innovation squandered by our broken systems.

It is no exaggeration to say that I'm writing this foreword during turbulent times, some may even say a moment of reckoning for our country. Centuries of racial injustice in every corner of society, from policing and criminal justice to education and work, are coming to a head. Protestors march in streets across the nation declaring a simple truth: "Black Lives Matter." It's time for those in power to start listening. Meanwhile, we are dealing with the most devastating health and economic crisis since the Great Depression, caused by the spread of COVID-19.

As of this writing, more than 40 million Americans have applied for unemployment benefits in four months, and our social systems are buckling under the weight. Of these newly unemployed workers, 80 percent are low-income, and the pandemic has had an outsized impact on people of color, women, and those without postsecondary degrees. In fact, one in four Black Americans has been laid off as a result of the crisis, compared to 15 percent of white Americans.[2] The truth is that these underlying disparities have existed for a long time, but we were just handed a magnifying glass to see them more clearly.

I spent more than a decade at the US Department of Labor tackling education and workforce disparities and challenges through policy, legislative, and regulatory initiatives across three presidential administrations. Feeling stifled by a system resistant to change, I did what very few federal officials did at the time: I left.

---

[1] National Center for Education Statistics. "Certificates and Degrees Conferred by Race/Ethnicity," The Condition of Education, 2017. https://nces.ed.gov/programs/coe/pdf/coe_svc.pdf.

[2] Emma Whitford, "People of Color, Disproportionately Affected by Pandemic, Expect to Need More Education If Laid Off, Survey Shows," *Inside Higher Ed,* April 23, 2020. https://www.insidehighered.com/news/2020/04/23/people-color-disproportionately-affected-pandemic-expect-need-more-education-if-laid.

That experience, and my subsequent decade at the nonprofit Jobs for the Future (JFF), shaped my philosophy toward education and workforce reform. At JFF, where I now serve as president and CEO—and where I proudly call Stephanie a colleague—we adopt a dual transformation approach to change with a renewed commitment to equity. *Making It* embodies this philosophy.

In order to reimagine education and work, we must embrace change from within our systems and drive change outside of them. Neither strategy is as effective alone as the two are in tandem. Often, within systems, there's little appetite for bold or disruptive thinking. But these structures are powerful tools for change and service delivery at scale. By leveraging existing systems while also working outside them, and investing in innovative solutions, we can make real, scalable progress and provide economic opportunity for all.

Making It examines what young people need to be ready for tomorrow's world with this approach in mind. A high school diploma, or even a bachelor's degree, is not enough for a young person to develop a thriving career. Stephanie disrupts this education paradigm, honestly and clearly laying out the currencies young people will need to succeed (not simply the degrees, though credentials are important), while also describing ways in which educators can build these currencies with the tools already at their disposal.

Many skills that I use on a daily basis in my current role are ones I learned on the job during my teenage years—from my stint as a "salad bar manager" at a Bonanza steakhouse to working retail at a men's clothing store on the Jersey Shore. And I was able, with the help of my "lifelines," as Stephanie calls them, to piece together these currencies in a way that built a path forward—largely in parallel to my academic experience.

For far too long, our education system has been disconnected from the world of work, which has had serious consequences for many young people, particularly those without the social capital needed to navigate the workforce. Young people today leave high school without the credentials or skills they need to succeed, and without a GPS to direct them to in-demand careers or to the pathways that will lead them there. Most college graduates also feel unprepared for the workforce, with little real-world experience under their belts but with mountains of student debt on their backs. The system needs reimagining from within and from without.

The CEOs with whom I work regularly tell me that they want problem solvers, critical thinkers, and collaborators, but our education system isn't equipping young people with these skills. Businesses want employees with technical skills, of course, but they also want people with the ability to adapt and learn, because today's jobs may not exist in 5 or 10 years as technology continues to evolve. In an age when automation is continuing to reshape the workplace, young people will need to prepare for multiple discrete jobs across their lifetimes, requiring them to constantly reskill. They will need to become lifelong learners, and Stephanie has designed solutions for this future that are practical, actionable, and universal.

In this time of rapid change, *Making It* provides a roadmap for those of us seeking to prepare young people—both inside and outside of the classroom—for the world of work. Whether you are a parent, teacher, administrator, or policy wonk, it's time to embrace a new model of education with an intentional focus on racial equity and equal opportunity that will help build a future that works.

Maria Flynn
President and CEO
JFF

INTRODUCTION

This book explores how today's kids and the world are changing, and what that means for what young people need to be ready for adulthood. Most schools, curriculums, and youth programs were not designed for this new reality. Instead, systems like public schools operate from outdated models meant to prepare farm kids to work in factories. Beyond farms and factories, our public schools were also designed for a white student body. Consequently, our school system consistently advantages white students over their Black and brown peers.

Today, young people are transitioning into an adult life full of rapid change and unpredictability. It is time for us to update our understanding of what young people need and upgrade their educational and preparatory experiences accordingly. Doing so gives us the opportunity to redesign education in ways that remove historic barriers to opportunity and harmful policies and practices; it also provides an opportunity to construct a more holistic approach to learning that is steeped in the real world and levels the playing field.

This Book Is for You

This book is for anyone who supports young people's learning and development. This includes those on the education frontlines—teachers, counselors, parents, and youth workers—and those running our schools, districts, and community programs, who make the policy and practice decisions that impact so many kids' lives and learning experiences.

When I taught and ran a school, I knew we were working off of outdated information, but I didn't have the time or resources to find what I needed to update our thinking and modernize practice. Knowing these real constraints, this book was designed to:

- Include information you need but don't have time to look for.
- Organize that information in ways that are easy to read and act on.
- Make this enjoyable to read, whether you take it on cover to cover or in pieces.

In Chapter 1, we consider today's kids—how they are wired by their experiences, what they care about, and what makes them so different from the rest of us. We see what it means that they don't know a world without high-speed internet and smartphones. We meet the recession-resilient high school graduating class of 2020, who entered kindergarten during the Great Recession and graduated high school during COVID-19. We come face-to-face with a generation of kids who crave safety and stability and hope for a steady job and good life.

In Chapter 2, we examine our rapidly changing world and workplace. We explore how machines, sheer momentum, and an evolving market are reshaping how we live, learn, and work. We consider the jobs and skills of the future, and the roles that artificial intelligence, augmented reality, and virtual reality will play in tomorrow's workplace. We wrap up with some predictions on what kinds of work young people will likely experience over their lifetimes.

The first part of the book makes it clear that our de facto "checklist for adulthood"—finish high school, go to college, graduate, get a job, make money, get promoted (or find a better job), retire, and live comfortably—no longer holds. Tomorrow's world is a vast and ever-evolving opportunity marketplace that demands certain life currencies to make it. These currencies are competencies, connections, credentials, and cash.

The second part of the book dives into these four currencies. Chapter 3 describes the competencies young people must develop before they transition into adulthood, including the abilities to focus, problem solve, relate, and engage with others. Chapter 4 examines the connections—relationships and social capital—young people rely on in school, at work, and in everyday life. Chapter 5 addresses the massive changes underway in the postsecondary education world. We will see what a modern high school diploma should include and consider which questions young people need to answer before choosing a postsecondary credential. In Chapter 6, we get honest about how much cash matters, but how little we talk about it in education. We look at the link between learning and living and see what young people need to get by and get ahead.

The final part of the book lays out five characteristics of currency-builders, that is, educators—inside and outside of the classroom—who transform the places and spaces where young people learn into currency-rich environments. You will find these characteristics work at home, at school, in the workplace, and in the community. They can be operationalized in-person, online, or both.

These currencies can be learned, earned, or inherited. America's long history of racism has made it harder for Black, brown, indigenous, and immigrant families to build and pass down currencies to their children. Generations of discrimination and struggle mean that their families often don't start out with enough financial or social capital. These young people have to work hard to make up the difference and, because of continued exclusionary practices, work harder than their white peers to accrue more.

Because of this, the currencies—along with the currency-building strategies presented in this book—must be viewed with a racial equity lens.

Bottom line: it is hardest for young people of color to make it in America. Our schools, workplaces, hospitals, and other systems were not designed with them in mind. This is only compounded when those young people have other experiences that push them farther to the margins. This might include being disabled, poor, or undocumented, experiencing housing instability, or being systems-involved—or even several of these experiences at once. These young people are forced to endure the universal stresses and challenges of today's world, while also taking on a whole other set of race- and experience-related challenges that make it much harder to succeed overall.

Let's Face It—the Future Is Now

I was finishing the first draft of this book when a bat in a Chinese meat market got someone sick and infected the world. Overnight, many of our households became home schools, and we were all reminded that school is much more than where kids go to get academic content. The pandemic illustrated how closely young people's quality of learning is tied to their quality of life. Right away, we saw kids with the most social and financial resources doing much better than their more isolated and cash-strapped peers. The year 2020 exposed the many ways a crisis can affect young people's current and future life trajectories.

Those growing up on America's social and economic fault lines—divides that continue to be marked by race and class—were hardest hit and most held back. COVID-19 illuminated the many ways that volatility, disparity, and disruption will define all kids' lives, and especially the most vulnerable.

What happens to young people today will impact what they are capable of as future workers and heads of households. Too often, we talk about the future of work but not tomorrow's workers. Or, we talk about the future of learning but not the changing workforce and economy. This book is an attempt to bring those conversations together.

A Few Other Considerations

Early into the writing process, I called my brother in a panic. He is a journalist and radio producer, and I needed his advice. My book research and interviews kept elevating the importance of mental health and youth development, but I was trying to write a book about education and preparation. He encouraged me to discuss those themes up front. So here they are.

It did not matter who I interviewed—young people, teachers, parents, policymakers, professors, employers, or pediatricians—everyone had two of the same concerns when we talked about preparing today's kids in tomorrow's world:

- **Today's kids are overloaded and overwhelmed.** If young people are too stressed, stretched, or sad to show up to school or work, they will not make it. This goes before and beyond the currencies and requires that we prioritize young people's mental health, identity development, individual experiences, stress management, and cognitive load. We have to get this right. The ability to manage constant overwhelm and overload will be their oxygen mask.

- **What we call "enrichment" or "extracurricular" is essential and expensive.** I was surprised by how often currencies are accrued by participating in the arts, athletics, camps, and clubs. In education, the past 20 years have focused on academic success; the next 20 need to include social and emotional development, as well as cognitive and physical fitness.

Finally, I was surprised to learn that many of today's kids will live to be at least 100. And yet, that is least true for children of color and those born into poverty. Too many of these children will not even make it past the first-quarter of life. If science says all children *could* have a 100-year-life, then we must shift how we talk about the future and youth readiness, committing to a new set of preparatory and protective factors—what I call currencies and currency-building strategies—that will make the prospect of a 100-year livable life more than a possibility.

PART I

A Changing World

CHAPTER 1

Today's Kids

My older son started asking for a smartphone in first grade. He seemed desperate and asked obsessively. By six, he was convinced he was the only kid in school without one. When I said no, he shifted gears and asked for a smart watch. He and his brother have grown up online and with digital devices in easy reach. Sometimes I think they feel as fondly about these devices as their beloved childhood stuffed animals, Fernando and Snuggles.

Early on, I had a failed attempt at laissez-faire parenting surrounding my kids' technology use. That changed when their older god-siblings spent a summer with us, and we suddenly catapulted from conversations about general "tech time" into complex conversations about online gaming and the safe use of social media. I was totally unprepared and sought counsel from Google and mom blogs. After deliberation, we said yes to just one game.

Everything was fine until my godson started talking about his online friends. He and I spent several hours reviewing his "friends'" profiles and found that most were adults who openly referenced drug use and sex. Somehow, all of them had been able to create accounts in the kids-only portal.

As if I wasn't Luddite enough already—and in a stroke of less-than-perfect parenting—I banned the game and hid the devices in places too high for the kids to reach. I justified my actions, pointing to the Silicon Valley parents who don't let their kids use iPads, sending them to tech-free schools and getting their nannies to leave cell phones at home.[1] I told myself that going tech-free was the right move, because smartphones might cause cancer[2] and too much social media might make my kids sad, sick, or lonely.[3]

That parenting moment may not have been my best, but I was worried and wanted to slow down the full immersion my kids have—often without me—into an online world—a world I don't always understand. It is a world of incredible access and opportunity, but also risk and exposure.

Digital Natives

Today's kids have a much different relationship with and need for technology than adults.

I was in middle school when my family got our first desktop computer. I have grown up with the release and rise of personal devices—experiencing the evolution from bulky desktops and "car phones," to more portable laptops and flip phones, and now to sleek and smart devices that are always with us.

Meanwhile, my kids were born into a world with technologies that were already smart, fast, thin, and available in a range of colors and sizes. They are digital natives. My older son, born in 2010, is three years younger than the iPhone, Twitter, Kindle, Airbnb, and Bitcoin.[4] He knew how to get to his favorite smartphone app before he could walk or talk.

---

[1] Nellie Bowles, "A Dark Consensus About Screens and Kids Begins to Emerge in Silicon Valley," *New York Times*, October 26, 2018, sec. Tech and Internet Culture. https://www.nytimes.com/2018/10/26/style/phones-children-silicon-valley.html.

[2] Chukwuma Muanya, "How Mobile Phones Cause Cancer, Depression," *The Guardian*, November 13, 2018, sec. Health. https://guardian.ng/features/how-mobile-phones-cause-cancer-depression/.

[3] Markham Heid, "We Need to Talk About Kids and Smartphones." *Time,* October 10, 2017, sec. Health Research. http://time.com/4974863/kids-smartphones-depression/.

[4] Thomas L. Friedman, *Thank You for Being Late: An Optimists Guide to Thriving in the Age of Accelerations*, 2nd ed. (Picador, 2016).

Here are some generational differences in common technology and tools between today's parents and their kids:

A Comparison of Childhood Technology Use

Today's Parents	Today's Kids
Encyclopedia Britannica	Siri and Alexa
Tetris	Minecraft and Roblox
Cassette tapes and CDs	Spotify and YouTube
Blockbuster	Netflix and Disney+
Department stores	Amazon
Landlines	Smartphones and watches
Folded notes	Snapchat and Instagram
Dial-up internet	Broadband WiFi

Disconnecting kids from devices can be as painful as separating them from a best friend. When my boys were little, we gave these meltdowns a name: the "Triple T"—a Technology Temper Tantrum. It generally involved a combination of shouting, crying, storming off, and sometimes lashing out with hands and feet. In our house, the Triple T was the worst when the boys had to suddenly power down a device, cutting them off from sudden short bursts of on-demand content. While the Triple T has changed over the years, I feel like it is still lurking in the background.

For adolescents, digital devices can be as important as a best friend, and as frequently used as a body part. My mom once asked a high school class what they would grab in a fire. Every single student said smartphone. Not one said family, pets, or photos. For today's kids, smartphones are a vital way to stay connected and plugged in.

Technology Dependence

This intense technology attachment has been studied by psychology professor Jean M. Twenge. She found that today's kids would rather be on their phone than with their families, and many confessed to liking digital devices more than people.[5] Twenge has dubbed this generation the "iGen."

---

[5] Jean M. Twenge, *IGen: Why Today's Super-Connected Kids Are Growing Up Less Rebellious, More Tolerant, Less Happy—and Completed Unprepared for Adulthood*and What That Means for the Rest of Us* (Simon and Schuster, 2017).

In her interviews, young people shared that they sleep with smartphones under pillows and wake up throughout the night to check for new notifications. Her surveys show that today's kids spend up to six hours a day on smart technologies—texting, on social media, online, and gaming.

My own conversations back that up. One mom told me about a niece who was having seizures brought on by the video games she was playing. Her parents were shocked by how hard it was for their daughter to give up those video games—even knowing that it was compromising her health and well-being.

While this is different from our childhoods, it may be similar to our work lives. According to my phone analytics, as a remote worker I spend three to four hours a day on my phone—some combination of calls, texting, and checking social media and email. Combine that with the amount of time I spend on my computer and I'm suddenly on par with, if not even more plugged in than today's kids. Since COVID-19, that time online has only increased. I'm now more dependent than ever on Zoom and other video technologies as well as online productivity platforms. Unfortunately, we don't know enough about what counts as too much tech and its long-term effects—especially for those who have been doing it since they were toddlers. The science simply hasn't caught up.

Technology Disparities

Technology dependence took on a whole new meaning when schools shut down because of COVID-19. Suddenly, continuous learning had to do with having continuous access to a digital device and the internet. Unfortunately, many were without. In extreme cases, young people were completely cut off.

One teacher told me that he showed up to work one day and was told to put together printed packets for his students. Teachers were being sent home for the rest of the year. His school was notoriously low-tech and underresourced, so his students were left with very little support and schooling during the shutdown.

I also heard from a number of district and school staff about how those first few weeks were spent as a mad dash to get digital devices to students who didn't have them. Often, even that was not enough. Many of those students lacked a strong enough internet signal to plug in, join class, and submit work. This will continue to be an issue until internet is seen as a utility instead of a commodity. For now, a connection and the resulting continuity of learning is only available to those who can afford it.

There are early indicators that the learning loss associated with the COVID-19 pandemic will be far worse for those who lacked the basic and smart technologies so many families, including mine, take for granted. The digital divide illuminated by COVID-19, exists across race, class, and geographic lines. Learning is toughest for students with the fewest resources, which now includes anyone without a strong or reliable digital connection.

Hyperconnectivity

Can any good come from this need for hyperconnectivity? Between 2006 and 2009, a team of researchers led by Don Tapscott set out to better understand young millennials (the generation before iGen). Their findings are described in the book *Grown Up Digital: How the Net Generation Is Changing Your World*. Tapscott's team found that when young people have ample access to technology, they seem to be more collaborative and able to get things done faster. Digital natives seem to be more informed on world affairs and current events than previous generations. Tapscott hoped that might contribute to an increased appreciation for diversity and more altruistic attitudes.

On the other hand, devices can also lead young people to find and engage in online communities and conversations that are divisive and harmful. There are cases where young people become radicalized through the internet, often without their parents or caretakers knowing. In extreme cases, these are the stories of lone shooters and young people who leave home to join a terrorist group. Then there are more common occurrences, such as a young person who bullies or is bullied online, or who gets hurt while trying to do a stunt shown on TikTok or SnapChat.

Although social media and virtual communities can have real drawbacks, these online mediums do give young people direct access to engage in issues and causes they care about, from petitions and protests to social and political campaigns. For most of today's kids, there is always the option to hop online to find or participate in almost anything they can imagine. We saw this kind of online youth activism really take root and flourish after the Parkland school shooting, throughout the #MeToo protests, and during the Ferguson protests and rise of the #BlackLives Matter movement.

COVID-19 brought on an even more recent and unexpected area of hyperconnectivity. Suddenly, young people had to shift their learning and socializing to be completely online. Devices became necessary conduits to the outside world, the way to keep up with friends and school.

Anecdotally, we have seen that young people responded to this change in a million different ways. There were stark differences across communities, schools, and even households. The switch was particularly painful for young people with disabilities and food insecurity who rely on school for life-sustaining services. Many of those supports could not be provided online or at a distance.

And while many young people found themselves more hyperconnected than ever, there were plenty of others who lacked a digital device or reliable internet connection. They were cut off from everything. For them, COVID-19 brought on both a physical and digital quarantine.

We won't understand the full ramifications of this crisis-induced switch for many years. I suspect there will be a strong relationship between how well someone does in life and how connected they were during the COVID-19 pandemic. Granted, connectivity will also mean their family was more likely to keep working, learning, getting groceries, applying for aid, and more.

At the end of the day, the concerns we have around young people's technology dependence and digital exposure may be shortsighted. I spoke with my colleague, Ichiro, who is comfortable and fluent in the digital world. While he's not a digital native, he can pass as one. As a result, he and his children can engage in in-person and online together.

This active engagement makes the transitions between virtual and real-world activities more fluid and seamless. In his house, there are no screen time limits because going in between worlds is a part of life. Amazingly, his kids don't suffer the same Technology Temper Tantrums that mine did, and he has found that his children get as excited to engage in the real world as they do to get online. Ichiro and his family give me hope that as we move into a future where children and parents are both digitally fluent—where being online feels less foreign and forbidden—there may be an increasing number of benefits to outweigh the risks.

Digital Footprints

Beyond hyperconnectivity, today's kids have a digital story that, for many, starts at birth. To be honest, if I could do it again, I would have been way more discriminating about which of my boys' milestones and moments I shared online. Like many, I posted and documented everything from first sonograms to birth pictures, videos of first foods, and funny stories. When my husband and I ran out of phone space for our videos, we uploaded them to YouTube. I've scaled back, but I still use social media as a way to share pictures, well wishes, and family announcements.

As a parent, I do it for convenience and because it is what most parents do. The problem is that I, and my parenting peers, inadvertently initiated a digital footprint for my children without their permission. I have given their image and information over to companies whose ethics and practices are increasingly being called into question. Every time I post their pictures and stories online, I give them over for sharing and future uses that are yet to be determined.

The data we put online is often shared and sold without our knowledge or consent, even if we have disabled sharing features. There is evidence that social media platforms, such as Facebook, have lost track and control of who has access to that information.[6]

This means our kids are facing even larger threats than adults posing as kids in online games or cyberbullying from their peers. They are also vulnerable to innumerable groups using their data and information to drive a bigger profit, targeting them for consumeristic means, or even using their information in nefarious ways, including cybercrimes and exploitation.

---

[6] Nicholas Confessore, Michael LaForigia, and Gabriel J.X. Dance, "Facebook's Data Sharing and Privacy Rules: 5 Takeaways From Our Investigation," *The New York Times*," December 18, 2019. https://www.nytimes.com/2018/12/18/us/politics/facebook-data-sharing-deals.html.

The digital footprint many of us started for our kids when they were babies will grow dramatically as they engage online. These digital interactions and impressions could even impact future hiring decisions.

In November 2018, the *Washington Post* published an article exposing how artificial intelligence (AI) is used to mine young people's online activity to determine whether they are suitable for certain jobs. The article, "Wanted: The 'Perfect Babysitter.' Must Pass AI Scan for Respect and Attitude,"[7] describes Predictim, an online service that determines whether a candidate is a "fit" based on scanning available social media posts by or about that person. The AI algorithms then generate an assessment that suggests whether the candidate is likely to be a good or bad employee, or if they are a drug abuser or have a bad attitude.

With today's kids spending so much time online, connecting with friends and constantly posting, they are unknowingly surrendering ownership of their moments and personal details to companies, including Apple, Facebook, TikTok, and Snapchat. Marry that with well-intended and naive parents (myself included), and you have digital natives whose names and digital memories are available and usable in ways that are still unfolding.[8]

Disruption Natives

Today's kids are digitally connected, dependent, and often digitally distracted. But what else?

Let's consider "today's kids" as anyone born in the twenty-first century. On the older end of the spectrum, you have young people born in the early 2000s. They were babies in the days after 9-11 and during the War on Terror. They were starting elementary school during the Great Recession and graduating high school in the first months of the COVID-19

---

[7] Drew Harwell, "Wanted: The 'Perfect Babysitter.' Must Pass AI Scan for Respect and Attitude," *The Washington Post,* November 23, 2018. https://www.washingtonpost.com/technology/2018/11/16/wanted-perfect-babysitter-must-pass-ai-scan-respect-attitude/?noredirect=on.
[8] Karen Weise, "Amazon Knows What You Buy. And It's Building a Big Ad Business From It," *The New York Times,* January 20, 2019, https://www.nytimes.com/2019/01/20/technology/amazon-ads-advertising.html.

pandemic. Their major life milestones are steeped in our nation's recent crises and aftermaths.

Their younger siblings—say, those born after 2007—were born after Osama bin Laden was killed by US Special Forces, during an Obama or Trump historic presidency, and after the advent of smartphones and social media. Their births were probably announced online, and they will not remember life without an ever-available digital assistant, such as Siri or Alexa.

Collectively, this is a generation of young people preoccupied with safety and stability, responding to a childhood defined by a relentless rotation of economic stress, public health concerns, racism, violence, and a changing climate. Today's kids are more than digital natives. They are disruption natives. They are seriously concerned for their lives and livelihoods. As a nurse practitioner once told me, we should call them the "survival generation."

As this survival generation goes to college and begins to work, they seem to be more pragmatic and cynical than their passionate and optimistic millennial older siblings. While millennials were cast as self-promoters and dreamers, today's kids are more interested in a good job and steady paycheck. While their upbringing primes them to be innovators and entrepreneurs, many prefer working for someone else, uninterested in the risks of starting their own thing.[9]

The work world awaiting these young people has proved their cynicism to be well-founded. In the midst of COVID-19, many college campuses are in disarray, and a huge number of those once-reliable first jobs—including work in restaurants, retail, and hospitality—have been decimated by the virus and the subsequent economic recession.

Diverse and Inclusive

Today's kids are also more racially and ethnically diverse than ever. Since 2007, most babies born in America have been Black or brown. That means that the majority of America's young people struggle under the oppressive

---

[9] Twenge, *IGen: Why Today's Super-Connected Kids Are Growing Up Less Rebellious, More Tolerant, Less Happy—and Completed Unprepared for Adulthood *and What That Means for the Rest of Us.*

smog of racism and bigotry. The growing movement among educators to become antiracist cannot slow or stop. While every educator should have cared about issues of racial equity before, today there is no excuse. Educators cannot claim to be committed to children's best interests and also unwilling to examine and improve practices and policies, ensuring that equity is being actively pursued or achieved.

Emerging research also shows that young people are increasingly fluid and open regarding gender and sexual orientation and more and more tolerant and inclusive of other differences experienced by historically marginalized groups.

Living between in-person and online worlds may be assisted by increasing exposure to different people, cultures, and communities—especially for those who live in rural or homogenous communities. Older kids and young adults can play video games or engage on social media with faraway friends and strangers from around the world. These changing dynamics, if supported by self-reflective and caring adults, could help today's kids to become more accepting of difference than any previous generation.

Growing Up in a Flat, Fast World

As *New York Times* journalist and author Thomas Friedman has claimed, today's kids live in a "flat" and "fast" world. They are used to instant connections that enable them to constantly check in and find what they need. Often, there are no waits, no commercials, and no lines. This includes asking Google or Alexa for homework help or to play a favorite song. For some, this means being able to call for a ride via ride-share app so they don't have to wait for the bus or a parent pick-up. For adults, this instant access and immediacy can be super disruptive and even dislocating. But for our kids, this is all they know.

Strong and Powerful

On Valentine's Day 2018, high school students in Parkland, Florida, showed up to school with heart-shaped balloons, teddy bears, and boxes of chocolates. Later that day, 19-year-old Nikolas Cruz shot and killed 17 people in the school, wounding another 14. In the weeks that followed, we saw what this flat, fast, and hyperconnected group of young people is capable of in times of crisis. Within days, these digital and disruption native rallied and transformed collective anger and grief into action. *Never Again MSD (#NeverAgain)* formed and initiated a viral spread that led to an estimated 800 youth-led marches, dubbed "March for Our Lives."

Just five weeks after the shooting, hundreds of thousands gathered in communities across the nation, calling for action against gun violence. Consider these words from Cameron, one of the Parkland students:

> *My generation—having spent our entire lives seeing mass shooting after mass shooting—has learned that our voices are powerful and our votes matter. We must educate ourselves and start conversations that keep our country moving forward and we will. We hereby promise to fix the broken system we've been forced into and create a better world for the generations to come. Don't worry, we've got this.*

Cameron's words and the March for Our Lives movement show us that beyond today's young people being pragmatic and skeptical, they are deeply powerful advocates and organizers, with a commitment to fix what's broken.

We have seen younger activists rising up—confronting racism, policing, climate change, and sexism; demanding that they be heard and taken seriously. Young people are organizing direct actions, starting online petitions, and generating fundraising campaigns for causes and people they care about. This is where the combination of their fear and fierceness really shine.

While they may not be the generation to start new companies and take economic risks, they are the generation to see the many ways their lives are on the line, and the many injustices pushing them down and holding them back. We must support them in whatever ways we can to achieve their demands for something different and better.

Long-time activist and entrepreneur Jeremy Heimans and nonprofit executive Henry Timms call this "New Power." While many of today's kids have been directly impacted by the most shameful parts of American life—violence, waste, hate—their hyperconnectivity, diversity, and penchant for social change has motivated them not only to learn about issues but to track them, report them in real time, and then to work together and with adults to make change happen.

Afraid for Their Lives

Our youngest ones are still too little to organize movements or take themselves to protests. However, their childhoods are being permanently shaped by the everyday safety and health concerns and heightened racial, political, and economic tensions rocking American society.

If we feel exhausted and drained by current events, imagine what it is doing to our kids. Look no further than my own children's experiences:

- The first time my older son rode a school bus was to practice evacuation procedures in case of a school shooting.
- One of my children came home from school in tears one day, saying he had lied about who he would "vote for" for president, fearing his friends' rejection.
- Growing up in St. Louis, my kids know what "Ferguson" was and worry about their Black family members getting shot and killed by the police.
- When my younger son was in preschool, he told me that if a school shooter showed up at school, he would crawl inside his backpack to stay safe.
- Both boys are living through a global pandemic, school shutdowns, and the biggest economic crisis since the Great Depression.
- Extreme weather and a changing climate mean that my boys have experienced terrifying storms, a slew of tornado warnings, super-hot summers, and future risks of weather-related disasters and damage.

Combine the stress and impact of global and national threats with the everyday stresses of life and you have a recipe for toxic stress, trauma, grief, and loss. This is hardest for young people who are marginalized because of their histories, identities, and life circumstances. For these young people, they experience compounded toxicity because of the constant reminders and messages that say they are bad, damaged, different, or don't belong.

Consider this quote from Lee Siegel's January 2, 2020, *New York Times* opinion piece, "Why Is America So Depressed?"[10]

> *All of this mental carnage is occurring at a time when decades of social and political divisions have set against each other Black and white, men and women, old and young. Beyond bitter social antagonisms, the country is racked by mass shootings, the mind-bending perils of the internet, revelations of widespread sexual predation, the worsening effects of climate change, virulent competition, the specter of antibiotic-resistant bacteria, grinding student debt and crises in housing, health care and higher education. The frightening environment helps cause depression, depression causes catastrophic thinking and makes the environment seem even more terrifying than it is.*

According to the *Center on the Developing Child* at Harvard University, toxic stress shows up whenever we experience prolonged adversity, including frequent exposure to violence and economic hardship. Toxic stress can trigger all kinds of developmental, learning, and health problems.

We are seeing this translate into increased rates of childhood anxiety, depression, and even suicide. In 2018, *TIME* magazine reported that from 2008 to 2018, suicidal behavior among children and youth had doubled.[11] That was before COVID-19 and the global recession. Being at home, being alone, and being separated from important supports and services has jeopardized the mental health of many young people, including many who never struggled before. This jump in mental health issues is backed by every conversation I have had with professionals working in mental health, schools, or colleges. We need to figure out a way to keep up with young people's skyrocketing mental health needs.

New Wiring

Being digital and disruption natives has evolved young people's basic wiring. As our own lives show, we are shaped by our experiences and

---

[10] Lee Siegel, "Why Is America So Depressed?" *The New York Times*, January 2, 2020. https://www.nytimes.com/2020/01/02/opinion/depression-america-trump.html?action=click&module=Opinion&pgtype=Homepage.

[11] James Ducharme, "More Kids Are Attempting and Thinking About Suicide: Study," *Time*, May 16, 2018. https://time.com/5279029/suicide-rates-rising-study/.

environments. Today's kids are growing up in a rapidly changing world, full of historic firsts. As a result, they don't just seem different, they are different. Their childhood experiences and ever-evolving environments are wiring them to learn, work, and operate in new ways.

First-Quarter Wiring

Although we are always learning and changing, there are two times in life when major developmental growth and transformation occurs: early childhood (birth to age 5) and adolescence (ages 10 to 26). These are the periods when the brain has the most *plasticity*, meaning it is continuously shaped and reshaped in response to stimuli and situations. Brain development, which determines how today's kids show up in tomorrow's world, is pretty well set after the first quarter of life.

From the time kids are born to the moment they enter school, they are forming the foundational skills that will be needed throughout their lives, from communication skills to emotional expression.[12] Once puberty hits, kids enter their second (and last) round of intense growth and development. This is when any unused wires are discarded. The brain consolidates and organizes into durable circuit boards, called neural networks. This is also when the front part of the brain fully develops—this part, called the frontal lobe, is responsible for "executive functioning."

Executive functioning is responsible for self-regulation—the ability to control thoughts, feelings, and actions—as well as critical and creative thinking, and the ability to reason and plan.[13] Strong and healthy communication, emotional expression, and executive functioning are among the most important things you can develop to prepare you for adulthood's complexity.

Short Circuits

In 2014, Daniel Levitin published *The Organized Brain: Thinking Straight in the Age of Information Overload*. It was one of the first books to explore what the never-ending onslaught of information is doing to all of us. Levitin calls

---

[12] Daniel J. Siegel and Tina Payne Bryson, *The Whole-Brain Child: 12 Proven Strategies to Nurture Your Child's Developing Mind* (Robinson, 2011).
[13] Frances E. Jensen and Amy Ellis Nutt, *The Teenage Brain: A Neuroscientist's Survival Guide to Raising Adolescents and Young Adults* (HarperCollinsPublishers, 2015).

this "information explosion" and describes it as a tax on our daily lives, one that leaves many of us feeling perpetually overwhelmed and exhausted.

We need to consider what it means that heightened neuroplasticity periods are happening to young people at the same time as they experience an information explosion. Today's kids are being wired and rewired during and by an explosive Information Age. As they mature, they will be bombarded by an ever-increasing set of demands and distractions. All of us, but especially kids, lack the cognitive capacity to pay attention to everything coming at us, filtering it for importance and urgency.

In a way, our brains are a bit like smartphones; the amount of information coming in is too much for our operating system (brain) to handle. When we are overloaded, things slow down and generate unanticipated errors. This is especially risky when it interrupts or disrupts learning and development.

It would be helpful if today's kids could upgrade for a speedier operating system with more storage capacity. And that just isn't possible. Our brains don't have enough space for all of the environmental and experiential stimuli being taken in. Unfortunately, we haven't found a way to exchange our brains for a better model. Instead, to survive in tomorrow's world, today's kids will need better and longer-lasting ways to absorb, process, and filter information; store and retrieve that information; as well as to learn what can be shut off or paused in order to avoid burnout, performance issues, or just breaking down.

Cognitive Load and Information Addiction

Today's kids need to develop strategies that help them to regularly power down and take breaks from their many distractions, notifications, and demands. They also need to be able to shift attention and tier priorities. These are coping mechanisms that will assist them with the compulsive need to be digitally connected and constantly updated. This temptation is probably why so many high schoolers sleep with their phones.

Research has shown that the same "feel good" and "fight or flight chemicals" people get from drugs, sex, and other rushes—like bungee jumping or riding a roller coaster[14]—are released when a device dings with

---

[14] Ibid.

a new message or notification. Some researchers believe this phenomenon is as intense as a crack addiction.[15]

Today's kids are not only being inundated by information but becoming addicted to it. One child therapist I spoke to has noticed that her younger clients seem constantly overstimulated and expect instant gratification. She thinks this is contributing to the rising rates of anxiety and depression, as well as attention and hyperactivity disorders. As an addiction counselor would tell you, being "restless, irritable, and discontented" is one of the telltale signs that someone is struggling with an addiction or dependency issue.

Overloaded Circuit Boards

Few things have a more devastating impact on a young person's wiring and development than the experience of being poor. Researchers have found that income inequality impairs brain development and suppresses executive functioning, including ever-important skills like self-regulation. Being poor is stressful and tends to trip important wires in the brain and body.[16] This is one reason why kids from wealthier families seem to have better language skills and classroom behavior. Those circuits responsible for quick thinking, strong communication language, and executive functioning are vital. These are the skills that are of increasing importance for employment and solving our most complex challenges.[17]

Kids already operate at capacity because of the amount of information coming at them, but when they also experience financial hardship, it pushes them to the fringes of their cognitive bandwidth. These young people live every day stressed and stretched to the max.

---

[15] Twenge, *IGen: Why Today's Super-Connected Kids Are Growing Up Less Rebellious, More Tolerant, Less Happy—and Completed Unprepared for Adulthood *and What That Means for the Rest of Us.*

[16] Ibid.

[17] Cassidy L. McDermott, Jakob Seidlitz, Ajay Nadig, et al., "Longitudinally Mapping Childhood Socioeconomic Status Associations with Cortical and Subcortical Morphology." *The Journal of Neuroscience*, February 20, 2019, 39 (8): 1365. https://doi.org/10.1523/JNEUROSCI.1808-18.2018.

How Today's Kids Compare with Each Other

In 2013, investigative reporter Amanda Ripley published *The Smartest Kids in the World: And How They Got That Way*. This book compared high schoolers in the United States, Finland, South Korea, and Poland, giving us a glimpse into some very different school experiences. Ripley understood that in a flat, fast world these children would one day compete for jobs and other opportunities. Two points from the book really stuck out to me as I considered what kids need for the future:

- While the US is wealthy, our kids are not doing the best academically. They lag behind kids in other wealthy countries, both in math and critical thinking. These abilities are in high-demand and growing importance among employers.
- American high school diplomas are not a reliable measure of readiness for postsecondary education and work. There are other countries that do a better job with the quality control of their diplomas and degrees.

Race and Class Differences

The same year Ripley published her book, Professor Jason Purnell and his research team at the Brown School of Social Work at Washington University in St. Louis, Missouri, released a dramatic story of opportunity disparities in St. Louis, the city where my children were born.

The story went like this: If you were born in Clayton, a mostly white and wealthy part of St. Louis County, you could expect to live up to 18 years longer than if you were born just nine miles down the road in North City, a mostly Black and poor part of the city. His team's 2014 report, *For the Sake of All*, illustrated how hard it can be for North City residents to get essential resources—from healthy food and safe spaces for children to play, to quality learning opportunities and healthcare. St. Louis has a long history of racial segregation, and today the results tell the story. Like many cities, St. Louis has opportunity gaps divided by neighborhood and ZIP code. This is a story that illustrates how and why life outcomes are predictive along racial, class, and neighborhood lines.[18]

---

[18] "For the Sake of All: A Report on the Health and Well-Being of African Americans in St. Louis and Why It Matters for Everyone." 2015. Washington University in St. Louis, Missouri.

Purnell and his team created a fictitious child, Jasmine, to help the community understand what this means for young people and families. While Jasmine can make her own choices, they are limited by her environment and experiences. How well she does in life has to do with what resources and supports she has. Jasmine's story rings true for millions of young people across the country. These are children who start out behind because of where they live and what resources and opportunities are available for them.

Across the US, economic opportunity is least available to young people who are poor, and those who are poor are disproportionately Black and brown. Professor Raj Chetty and his research team at Harvard University have demonstrated this in their "Opportunity Atlas,"[19] which maps neighborhoods—by ZIP code—to household income, race, gender, and opportunity. He and his team have demonstrated that in the United States, a few blocks, income level, or race, can make life-altering differences in what it takes to make it.[20]

Making It in an Unfair and Unjust World

Undoing and correcting the persistent structural and systemic inequities that harm and hold back so many of today's kids is some of the most important work there is. And, as that is happening, we need to figure out ways to help young people make it in a world that is still unfair and inequitable.

The kind of education and economic justice we need is desired, but not guaranteed. Because of this, all educators must focus on figuring out what each kid personally needs to make it—and this is different, depending on the young person, where they live, what challenges they face, and what opportunities they have access to.

---

[19] Opportunity Insights and US Census Bureau, "The Opportunity Atlas," accessed May 27, 2020. https://opportunityatlas.org/.
[20] Raj Chetty, John Friedman, Nathaniel Hendren, Maggie Jones, and Sonya Porter, "The Opportunity Atlas: Mapping the Childhood Roots of Social Mobility," *CES-18-42*, September 2018.

CHAPTER 2

Tomorrow's World

I have not been to the grocery store in years. I rely on online shopping apps, choosing to pay others to shop for me. Initially, it was a one-year Christmas gift I bought myself. I get secret pleasure out of the apps telling me how many hours I have saved by using their services instead of going to the store.

If someone had told me a few years ago that soon I would pay a random stranger to shop for me and then come to my house, I would have said they were crazy. Now, I don't give a second thought to sharing my address and grocery list in exchange for getting some of my weekend back or—in the case of the COVID-19—staying safe at home. I have gotten pretty good at outsourcing my shopping needs and am now pretty reliant on these services. Whatever I can't get online, I try to get using "drive-up" or "curbside" assistance.

For now, my groceries get picked up and delivered by a person. I suspect that will change. Robots already work in the warehouse to find what I have ordered on Amazon. If I need to make a return, I do it online, without human interaction. Across the pond, online stores are even more popular. Ocado is a British online supermarket that has automated most routine tasks. Robots and humans work side by side, but most processing tasks are taken care of by machines, not people. Ocado processes some 3.5 million items each week. At the same time, Amazon and others are beginning to experiment with drone delivery services—one day everything from packages to pizza might be dropped by drone to your front door.

Each time I purchase something on an online shopping platform I fuel a man-and-machine powered workforce. This is where humans and technology operate as a unit to make or deliver a product or provide a service. While this relationship has existed since the Industrial Revolution, or longer if we consider cruder machines, I think emerging technologies such as intelligent robots, 3D printers, drones, and self-driving vehicles take this man-and-machine relationship to a whole new level.

In the case of my shopping apps, I use tech to place my order, transact payment, get assigned a shopper, track shopping progress, and keep an easy-to-access inventory of what I buy. I rely on a person to get groceries or goods and drop them off at my house. As the innovation happening at Ocado reveals, this human-assigned task might one day be automated.

In tomorrow's world, our most routine work tasks will shift from being done by bodies to bots. And with the way technology is advancing, some of our more complicated work may also become a robot's job.

Three Forces Shaping Tomorrow's World

My decision to use gig services and online shopping reveals more than a desperate attempt for a busy mom to save time and stay safe during a pandemic. It also illuminates three powerful forces, which are reshaping how we live, learn, and work.

- **Machines.** These are technologies, including robots, augmented and virtual reality, and artificial intelligence. To make it, today's kids need to learn how to work alongside machines, and—for some—how to make and improve them. In tomorrow's world, workers will need to contribute to the workforce in ways that are so fundamentally human that they are difficult, if not impossible, to automate.
- **Momentum.** This is the rate of change. Futurists, analysts, and everyday people agree—everything is changing so fast it is hard to

keep up. Momentum is where acceleration, innovation, and global competition live. Today's kids are growing up in an on-demand world and constantly operate at maximum cognitive capacity. Tomorrow's world will be even faster, and they will need ways to keep up and keep moving.

- **Markets.** These days, the way the world works and the way we work is complex and ever-changing. How we produce and consume is changing. People live longer, sometimes spending 60 years or more in the workforce. Companies are outsourcing, reimagining, and getting rid of certain jobs. As we get deeper into the twenty-first century we will transition from a knowledge economy to a learning economy. Today's kids are tomorrow's workforce. They must be able to continuously learn and recreate their working selves, updating and upgrading along the way.

These forces make the future hard to predict. Today's kids are growing up in exciting and dangerous times. Technological advances have the potential to solve some of our most intractable problems—drones that send food to disaster victims, cures for deadly diseases, solutions for climate change, transplant organs created on 3D printers—but these advances also open us up to new risks that we are not ready to respond to—cyberterrorism, super viruses, the rise of radical and widespread terrorist groups, and the illegal purchasing and printing of weapons.

This is a world that Darren Walker, president of the Ford Foundation, has described as ". . . on edge and off kilter, more precarious and less predictable."

As we move forward, robots will take many jobs but create many more. Markets will keep shifting and transforming, and there will be no shortage of work to be done. The question is, will kids have what they need to be ready for it? To succeed, young people will need to become innovators and disrupters, builders and rebuilders, caregivers and creators.

Machines

*These are emerging technologies, including robots, augmented and
virtual reality, and artificial intelligence. To make it, today's kids
need to learn how to work alongside machines, and—for some—how to
make and improve them. In tomorrow's world, workers will need to
contribute to the workforce in ways that are so fundamentally human
that they are difficult, if not impossible, to automate.*

Jennifer Silva is a gifted pediatric cardiologist and force of life. A
working mom of two, Jenn somehow manages a super-high-stress job
and parenting with endless energy and vision. She sees patients, lectures,
researches, and runs a department at St. Louis Children's Hospital for kids
with heart rhythm and electrical issues. She also founded a tech start-up—
SentiAR—with her husband. Together, they are using augmented reality
to enable doctors to project holograms of their patients' hearts in the
procedure room. By working with projected images, cardiologists can use
a risk-free tool to better understand, see, and fix whatever is wrong.

I know Jenn because my boys are her patients. They see Jenn once a
year, and I thank my lucky stars that we live close enough to St. Louis
for her to be their doctor. In my opinion, she is one of those magical
practitioners who makes you feel like family. She is warm and loving,
remembering nicknames and fun facts, full of free hugs and good advice.
All of this with the fact that she knows what she's talking about. This
combination facilitates tremendous trust. Super important when you are
dealing with kids' hearts.

I interviewed Jenn to learn more about her experience and predictions
about the future of work, as a medical doctor and tech entrepreneur, as
well as a working mom with kids the same age as my boys. She left me
optimistic. While robots might come for many of our jobs, she believes
they will also spur the creation of many new ones.

In the best version of man-and-machine, today's kids will become
workers who are better at what they do, embracing a high-tech, high-
touch orientation. They will become doctors who save more lives, teachers
who better educate students, advocates who organize more people, and

leaders who produce optimal results. In that version of the future, today's kids will not have to suffer in mindless and routine roles and will be much more likely to work in positions that demand creativity, critical thinking, curiosity, and compassion.

Jenn speaks to these possibilities like a modern-day prophet—explaining how we can use and build technologies, particularly augmented reality, to give doctors superhero abilities in the operating room. She, her husband, and their team use tech to solve the problems they could not alleviate on their own. She knew she would be a better doctor if only she could see her patients' hearts, simulating what would happen if she cut here, or moved over there. I can only imagine going inside little bodies, with worried parents in the waiting room. In those moments, there is no room for experimenting, because errors can be fatal, and children's lives are on the line.

A few years ago, Jenn's husband attended a meeting at Microsoft and found what his wife needed. Microsoft was showcasing an augmented reality technology where a person puts on a "holo-lens" (big bug-eyed-looking goggles) that projects a hologram that can be touched and played with. He immediately knew that this same technology could be used to create a holo-lens for Jenn and other pediatric cardiologists. Since then, she and her husband have been working to prototype that very product.

I was curious to see what Jenn thinks new technologies, like hers, mean for future doctors and nurses. Would it be possible, let's say, for their jobs to be done by robots one day? Some say it is.

She doesn't see it as an either-or proposition. From her perspective, technology—from single-task machines, such as defibrillators and pace-makers; to augmented and virtual reality, such as her holo-lens; to artificial intelligence that takes and analyzes huge amounts of data—works best with a human touch. Human work is made stronger by the predictability, reliability, and analytic capabilities of tech; and machine work is most useful when it is connected to human ingenuity and curiosity.

Before we wrapped up our conversation, Jenn reminded me what matters most: in an emergency situation, I would always choose her to keep my boys alive. I cannot fathom going through that with a robot. At the same time, it would be unforgivable if she failed because of a decision to not use whatever technology was available to take care of my kids.

From Bodies to Bots

Jenn is not the only one finding new ways to use technology in the work-place. Across the globe, innovators and employers are experimenting with how tech can reduce costs, while improving efficiency and effective-ness. This is not new. Consider the Industrial Revolution—a time when the steam engine led to mass production. Or what about the invention of home appliances, such as the laundry machine or dishwasher? We are always after new ways for technology to make our lives easier, save us time, and take on tasks we'd rather not do.

Through the years, people have learned that machines perform best when doing the routine and mundane. This might be a simple task (wash the dishes), or something more complex, like analyzing information in search of patterns that produce predictions. For now, machines still need humans to program, fix, and improve them.

Automation is whenever technology takes over a traditionally human role or task. Automation is happening faster and more often these days. There is pretty good consensus that because of this, the working world will look dramatically different from the one we have now, likely within only a few decades.

To put it in perspective, consider the December 2017 report by McKinsey & Company: *Jobs Lost, Jobs Gained: Workforce Transitions in a Time of Automation*. This report described the scope of automation and the ways in which it is upending how we work. If the predictions made by McKinsey come true, then by 2030, somewhere between 75 and 375 million work-ers will have to leave or change jobs because of automation. COVID-19 may have only accelerated this, potentially making these numbers higher. All of us will feel the effects and need to prepare ourselves. Young people should be taught to anticipate these shifts and then how to pivot or adapt.

The robots are not coming. They are here, with more on the way. Right now, they are taking over jobs that require fewer skills—where people do the same thing over and over—including stocking shelves, screwing on lids, taking orders, filing claims, and flipping burgers. Self-driving cars are not far behind, and one day we may see machines take the place of truck drivers, postal workers, and taxi drivers. Eventually, artificial intelligence will be smart and cheap enough to become our "Alexa" accountant, law clerk, or research analyst. For young people, this will be the only world of work they know.

Machines That Do

All day long I rely on machines, from simple to smart. In the morning, I wake up and fully expect my coffeemaker to work. My breakfast foods are taken out of the fridge and cooked using the stove and toaster. My family relies on our car to get around and my phone and laptop make remote work possible. In my home office, I turn on my humidifier and space heater in the winter and air conditioner in the summer.

Throughout the day I alternate between technologies. From my home in the Midwest, tucked down a quarter-mile drive, I can connect with whomever I want, no matter where they are in the world. In between work calls, I sometimes do the laundry or buy something online.

In the workplace, simple machines handle many back-office and assembly-line tasks. Taxes and making deposits no longer require account-ants and brick-and-mortar banks. Factory floors are now checkered with a mix of human and robot workers. For now, human workers handle the unpredictable or delicate (for example, handling and inspecting an orange or egg) and robots handle the less breakable and more predictable.

Machines are also more than robots. They are the technology analyzing our data, keeping us on task, and powering our grids. The electricity in my house is connected to a giant server somewhere else. My organization will hire fewer office managers but invest more in online project and knowledge management platforms. All of us who have worked remotely or at a distance, particularly since COVID-19 started, have relied on some level of tech and machines to get by.

Machines That Learn

Go to YouTube and search for "Sophia Robot." She is a social robot created by former Disney Imagineer David Hanson. Take some time to watch a few of the videos that come up. If you are like me and my boys, you'll be amazed. Sophia is an eerily lifelike robot—beautiful, with features modeled after Audrey Hepburn and the creator's wife. She has become a real public figure and seems to get smarter and more human every day. Sophia has been on *Good Morning America* and the covers of *ELLE* and *Cosmopolitan* magazines; she has addressed the United Nations, made jokes with Jimmy Fallon on *The Tonight Show,* and been granted Saudi Arabian citizenship (the first robot to become a citizen).

She doesn't just seem to be getting smarter and more human—Sophia is actually learning how to be more like us with every interaction she has. She is programmed to continuously learn and self-upgrade. She has man-made neural networks that enable her to gather and process data and look for patterns in order to behave and speak like those around her. Sophia is powered by *artificial intelligence* (AI). AI is a catch-all term for technology that performs something we consider to be a human characteristic, function, or skill. While AI used to be confined to science fiction, it is increasingly a part of how employers do business. When today's kids enter the workforce, they will be constant creators of and collaborators with AI.

AI does not always look like a beautiful movie star. More often, this intelligence lives "in the cloud" or in big data sets.

Machines Like Us

My family loves the Pixar *Incredibles* movies, and these movies are full of AI. It is hard to believe that there were 14 years between *Incredibles I* and *II,* but the gap is obvious when you see the difference in animation between both films. The animation in the second movie was so lifelike. The characters' facial expressions and movements looked truly human— except, of course, for the demonstration of superhero strength, stretch, invisibility, speed, and fire.

These movies remind me of a conversation I had with my husband's college roommate, Darren. After finishing his undergraduate degree, Darren enrolled in a doctoral program at Princeton University, where he studied biology and robotics. Today he works for ExxonMobil, where he is trying to find ways to optimize how we produce and consume energy. One day, Darren was trying to get my husband and me to understand the possibilities of robotics. He told us that engineers look to the natural world and how it's reproduced by movie animators, especially Disney and DreamWorks, to imagine what's possible. These extreme creatives and innovators operate on what Jenn Silva called the "intellectual edge," constantly stretching reality by using serious science to generate real breakthroughs in animation, artificial intelligence, and augmented and virtual reality.

Making Magic

The Disney Research website unpacks these engineering and robotics possibilities that make our beloved family movies so fun to watch. Disney Research has undertaken studies and written publications on uber-technical topics, like how to create human-like teeth, jaw movements, facial expressions, and even how to operate artificial muscles. If you have gone to Disney or Universal Studios, you may have experienced how realistic their robots can be. Movements are increasingly lifelike, and facial expressions are almost identical to our own. Behind the costumes, Disney's robots are running on digital neural connections, which are increasingly similar to our own.

Japanese Nursebots

In Japan, a pretty massive experiment is underway, which will test whether these more humanlike robots can help our households. The Japanese have long lifespans and low birth rates, which has led to a number of lonely, older adults. Enter, social companion robots. There are tens of thousands of them in use already. Social companion robots are life-sized and touchable, and programmed to remind owners to do things—including taking medicine, eating, turning off the stove, or getting in the shower.

With artificial intelligence and internet access, these robots can engage with us, answering questions about the weather, playing music, saying good morning, and answering trivia. This is exactly what Darren was talking about. Especially because, in this case, these social companion robots seem a lot like the "Nursebot" main character, Baymax, in one of our family's other favorite movies, Disney's *Big Hero 6*.

These types of machines will make young people pioneers in new technology and man-and-machine ethics.[1] Sophia and Japanese nursebots make it easy to imagine a future where humanoid robots offer concierge services at hotels, in-home nursing, companionship, cleaning services, shopping assistance, and even full-service dining. As artificial intelligence continues to get smarter, these machines will become more common in professions most of us assumed would always be held by humans, including jobs in medicine, law, and research.

Today's Kids and Machines: A Tech-Touch Relationship

In the future, workers will need to be comfortable with machines and able to work with, on, and for them every day. They will need to be able to get jobs that demand more than routinized tasks, because those jobs will likely be automated. They will also need strategies to navigate between in-person and digital worlds, able to work alongside artificial intelligence in addition to simpler technologies.

It's possible that technology will further segregate tomorrow's work-force between the technology haves and have-nots. Likely, this segregation will cut across racial and class lines. The haves will be a small group, highly educated and trained in specialized, niche professions. They will enjoy new opportunities and rising wages because they are most needed, fluent, comfortable, adaptive, and productive in the digital world. The have-nots—the possible majority—will be those who are lower-skilled with less access to technology and digital tools, employed in jobs at risk of technological disruption, dislocation, and automation.[2]

To elevate future employability and economic advancement, today's kids need to be building their digital and human skills right now. This only intensifies the urgent need to get all young people digitally connected.

---

[1] Paul R. Daugherty and James H Wilson, *Human + Machine: Reimagining Work in the Age of AI* (Harvard Business Review Press, 2018).
[2] Eduardo Porter, "Tech Is Splitting the US Work Force in Two," *The New York Times*, February 4, 2019. https://www.nytimes.com/2019/02/04/business/economy/productivity-inequality-wages.html.

Momentum

*This is the rate of change. Futurists, analysts, and everyday
people agree—everything is changing so fast it is hard to keep up.
Momentum is where acceleration, innovation, and global competition
live. Today's kids are growing up in an on-demand world and
constantly operate at maximum cognitive capacity. Tomorrow's
world will be even faster, and they will need ways to keep up and
keep moving.*

Imagine you spent your earliest years on a farm. Your family grew and
harvested your own food. There were no grocery stores or restaurants. My
online shopping habits, unfathomable. What you ate, and how much, had
to do with the weather and how hard you worked.

When you were a teen, a grocery store opened up nearby. Your family
slowly let go of farm life and embraced the convenience and selection
promised by the grocery store. By the time you turned 20, stores and
restaurants dotted the main road in town. Now your family went out to
eat and shopped at places based on personal preferences.

Around 23 or 24, your mom called to tell you she signed up for a meal
subscription service called Blue Apron. She explained that she would no
longer have to run to the store during the week and the service would
deliver pre-portioned ingredients and recipes directly to the house. By this
point, your family's farm had been sectioned into quarter-acre lots and sold
off to a development company. New homes were popping up every day.

On your 25th birthday, your Mom cooked *seared chicken & goat
cheese mashed potatoes with fig butter-glazed carrots* from Blue Apron and
joked with you about the old days, back when your family had to grow
your own food.

This is the story Paul Gaffney told me to help me understand why
things feel like they are changing so fast and so much. Paul is the chief
technology officer at Kohl's. He previously held leadership positions at
Dick's Sporting Goods and The Home Depot. He is a former school board
member, raised by educators and married to one. According to Paul, it is
not your imagination; everything really is moving faster than ever.

Paul describes this as a time of widespread conceptual compression. This is the underlying principle in the story of moving from agrarian life to Blue Apron over the course of several years rather than several centuries. Information and ideas used to be owned and hoarded, spreading slowly because people held them proprietarily. Then in the 1990s, open-source technology emerged—think Wikipedia—and suddenly information was free, available, and changeable to anyone with an internet connection. In an instant, we could directly contribute to each other's ideas and get and share information.

This massive sharing and storing of information happened during what Paul refers to as an "earth-shifting event" in 1991—that is, when Linus Torvalds, a Finnish American software engineer, created the Linux kernel. Linux created a way for people to work together on software without needing a third party, privacy guardrails, or pay. Today, this open sourcing has become a cultural norm. We are living in an Open Source Society where we are able to actively co-create our futures, crowdsource information, and find virtually whatever information we need for free.

In an Open Source Society, previously proprietary information is suddenly free and accessible. We can use social media to find a plumber, pediatrician, or parenting advice. Most video games are open source, like Minecraft, enabling groups of strangers to work together to build something, become a community, or weave a storyline.

We have been launched from a metaphoric farm to a nearly assembled table, in a fraction of the time it should have taken, in large part, because everyone is building off of someone else's thinking or efforts. This cycle of change has led to a compulsion to be constantly plugged in, in the loop, and catching up. The benefit is, we get to be a part of creating better solutions, faster (for example, a single-day hackathon used to generate national security solutions); the risk is that slowing down puts you in jeopardy of falling behind, because everything is moving so fast.

An Open Source Society

Living in an Open Source Society means that anyone, from an aspiring entrepreneur in rural Wyoming to a business executive in Pittsburgh, Pennsylvania, can contribute to solving the same problem. Some of the researchers and professors I spoke with think that tomorrow's world will no longer need patents, longitudinal research studies, or lengthy drug trials. All of these are now viewed as outdated because they take such a long time. Before some drugs and products are approved for the market, they already need to be revised. Or, something new and better has been invented during the wait.

This is a way of living that feels at once exposed and participatory. Every day the world seems faster, smaller, busier, and—frankly—a little more overwhelming.

Here's a quick list of Open Source Society characteristics. These are examples of how momentum is shifting our behaviors, cultures, and values.

CHARACTERISTICS OF OUR OPEN SOURCE SOCIETY

Example	Description
#Hashtag Activism	#BlackLivesMatter. #MeToo. #ASLiceBucket Challenge. #UmbrellaRevolution. Today, social change and movement-making can grow and transform with unprecedented speed and virality because of hashtags along with no-cost and distributed social media engagement. #Hashtag activism can shift power from the abuser to the victim, the majority to the marginalized. It is a hugely participatory and decentralized phenomenon, made possible by our hyperconnectivity.
Fortnite Dances	If you have seen kids *floss* or *take the L* (to me, "taking the L" looks like a combination of the "Loser" sign and "pee-pee" dance) then you have seen Fortnite's viral dance moves. It's a cultural phenomenon started in the online multiplayer video game, which grosses more than $120 million in monthly sales.[3] The virality has extended Fortnite far beyond the video game to include kids across the world who have dance competitions on playgrounds and in classrooms.

(Continued)

---

[3] Sarah L. Kaufman, "The Dances in 'Fortnite' Have Become Nearly as Contagious as the Game," *The Washington Post*, September 10, 2018. https://www.washingtonpost.com/news/arts-and-entertainment/wp/2018/09/10/the-dances-in-fortnite-have-become-nearly-as-contagious-as-the-game/?noredirect=on&utm_term=.3767dbe38812.

CHARACTERISTICS OF OUR OPEN SOURCE SOCIETY

Example	Description
Viral Videos	A baby panda sneezing. A baby born deaf hearing his mother for the first time. A dog greeting his owner after a military deployment. These videos capture our hearts, and the hearts of millions of others. Mostly shot by personal devices, these videos get shared, tagged, and shared again. The speed of sharing is made exponentially faster by back-end algorithms that seem to sense the viral potential, suddenly lifting up these clips as trending at the top of your personal news feeds.
FOMO	Heard of FOMO? This acronym for "fear of missing out" defines our Open Source Society and is often used to describe the constant need to check phones and feeds, in an effort to stay in the know. FOMO can cause anxiety, stress, and compulsive thinking. People sometimes panic when they are separated from their digital devices.
Momo	Don't confuse FOMO for Momo. The Momo Challenge was a viral scare that got me, our school principal, and many others. The *New York Times* called it the "terror of parenting in the age of YouTube." Momo was a supposed creepy monster popping up on kids' YouTube videos, telling them to do life-threatening things and not tell their parents. Parents and educators across America had serious conversations with their kids in an effort to prevent possible suicide-by-Momo-influence. Turns out, it was fake news!

Momentum can initiate everything from laughter caused by viral videos and funny dance moves, to disaster caused by skyrocketing stress levels, new security threats, and climate concerns. And momentum just keeps speeding up.

Paul's discussion of conceptual compression shows how acceleration can transform business, industry, the economy, and the environment. Writing this book is a great example of how this happens. I was finishing my first draft when COVID-19 hit. Suddenly the world had changed, and I needed to revise. In between the first and final versions, a new wave of racial violence and uprisings took place, but this time with unprecedented white engagement and corporate commitments to change. Time to revise again. I am submitting my manuscript before schools reopen, before the next national election, and before the end of the COVID-19 pandemic. By the time it hits bookstores, there may be no physical bookstores left. There may be no in-person book talks. There will already be more changes and lessons to communicate to readers (achievable, thankfully, by using social media and a website). Today, everything needs constant review, revision, updates, or upgrades. Disruption, acceleration, and innovation are the seeming bedrocks of our new economy.

Game Rules

To work and lead in this fast world, today's kids need to be able to think and operate in new ways.

Consider the game *Disruptus*. Someone pulls a card, which has a picture of a common item. You roll the dice and, depending on what you roll, players have one minute to either improve or transform the object in the picture, or think of an entirely new way of accomplishing the task the object is meant to do.

Let's say the card is a picture of an ironing board. Depending on the turn, you might transform the ironing board into a standing desk; create a more modern, better ironing board; or disrupt the concept of ironing and think of a different way to remove wrinkles from your clothes. Tomorrow's economy is a bit like a real-life version of *Disruptus*.

Volatility in an Open Source Society

Privacy breaches that require credit monitoring and password changes. Fires in California with smoke that reaches Canada. Terrorist cells using online propaganda and recruiters to convince young people to leave home for a dangerous cause. Pandemics, superbugs, and the rapid spread of disease.

Tomorrow's world is one that will have as much volatility as virality. Today's kids must be just as prepared for the spread of things that cause harm as for the scale of solutions that help.

The world is not only faster but seemingly scarier. This is partly because we know more about what is happening, thanks to our 24/7 news cycle and the internet. And realistically, we are up against some really frightening realities and possibilities.

Climate volatility and extreme weather bring numerous and growing threats. Here in the Midwest, severe storms feel more like tornadoes. Vertical wind shafts take down trees and powerlines. Environmental changes are reshaping our geography, forcing economic transitions, and global migrations.[4] Every year seems to bring more severe natural disasters, each broadcast as a historic first—heatwaves, wildfires, cold spells, hurricanes, illnesses, and more.

Today's kids are inheriting a world that is more temperamental than ever. According to the *Fourth National Climate Assessment,* released in November 2018, climate change threatens America's economic health, infrastructure and property, essential services, clean water and energy, and our personal health. These changes are capable of and already producing economic recessions, food shortages, pandemics, and natural disasters. And these changes are speeding up. Because of this, tomorrow might include major population shifts from climate-related migrations and moves. Entire communities could be displaced. Today's kids will need the resilience and resources to respond and recover from any number of destructive disasters and crises.[5]

There is also cultural volatility. Today's kids are growing up with mounting tensions and more visible violence within and between countries and communities as well as across racial, family, and political lines. Faith in government and public institutions is wavering.

All of this makes the world feel like a tinder box. Climate and cultural volatility threaten our homes, safety, connections, and quality of life. Surviving requires being well-resourced, supported, and capable of carrying on when faced with the more dangerous parts of momentum.

We will need young people to build careers tackling and addressing these issues. The future needs community builders, organizers, activists,

---

[4] Katherine Prince, Jason Swanson, Katie King, and Andrea Saveri, *Navigating the Future of Learning.* KnowledgeWorks, 2018. https://knowledgeworks.org/resources/forecast-5/.
[5] Ibid.

and social champions who grow new "high-value" fields that can address our most pressing environmental, economic, and social challenges.

Overloaded and Overwhelmed

Access to information, increased stress, and mounting demands for our time and attention have left many feeling chronically overloaded and overwhelmed. Busyness is recognized as a badge of honor. A full calendar, rather than vacations and leisure, now a status symbol.[6] The World Health Organization (WHO) has classified burnout as a diagnosable syndrome and occupational phenomenon. For many, the feeling of having too much going on and too much to deal with has only intensified under the pressures and uncertainty brought on by COVID-19.

Match the symptoms of our Open Source Society with this legitimate time scarcity, and you end up with a phenomenon I call *the overwhelm.*

Tomorrow's world will not only be faster and scarier, it has the potential to be so overwhelming that it debilitates. The overwhelm goes beyond schedules. It includes the emotional and mental strain we all contend with, as well as the fear of the unknown. Constant demands on time and attention make it hard to figure out what to focus on and how to concentrate. To make it, young people will need to be able to connect and disconnect at will, as well as practice concentration in the midst of intense distraction.

To get perspective, I reached out to Cal Newport, bestselling author of *Deep Work* and *Digital Minimalism,* and—lucky for me—someone I grew up with. It was helpful to talk about this with him, especially since our kids are similar ages and we have the shared experience of growing up in the same hometown.

According to Cal, the best thing we can do to prepare kids for tomorrow's world is teach them how to concentrate, even when they are contending with a million different distractions. Making it will require being able to manage what we give time and attention to. Young people will need to learn how to do this early on, and it will be a skill that needs plenty of practice and use over time.

---

[6] Celeste Headlee, *Do Nothing: How to Break Away from Overworking, Overdoing, and Underliving* (Harmony Books, 2020).

Slow and Steady Wins the Race

In a fast and Open Source Society, the turtle wins the race. Unattended overload and overwhelm will lead to lost productivity, anxiety, stress, and burnout. Combine that with virality and volatility, and today's kids run the risk of living a life feeling perpetually frantic and frayed. Finding ways to slow down, concentrate, and unplug will be paramount.

Since today's kids are growing up amidst the momentum, it is possible that by adulthood, they will have had enough. Cal believes they may be the ones to find ways to effectively manage the frenzy and reduce the overwhelm. In his research, he has found that it's common for societies to initially struggle to stay organized and manage workflow during times like these, periods of massive shifts and technological change.

Markets

These days, the way the world works and the way we work is complex and ever-changing. How we produce and consume is changing. People live longer, sometimes spending 60 years or more in the workforce. Companies are outsourcing, reimagining, and getting rid of certain jobs. As we get deeper into the twenty-first century we will transition from a knowledge economy to a learning economy. Today's kids are tomorrow's workforce. They must be able to continuously learn and recreate their working selves, updating and upgrading along the way.

I met Roger the day I decided to trade in my minivan. He was working at our local car dealership and grew up just a few miles down the road. His family had a 250-acre dairy farm, and he remembers the days when our community was far more rural than it is today. For years, his family farmed his land and provided neighbors with ice cream and milk in glass jars. Each day Roger would wake up before dawn to milk the cows and be back out at dusk to milk them again. He never imagined anything different.

Then a few years ago, robots were brought onto the farm. They took over milking the cows. For the first time, Roger could sleep in or stay out late into the evening. His family could take vacations, no longer subject to a grueling 12 hours per day, 7 days per week milking cycle. Soon after the robots took over milking, Roger realized there was nothing left for him to do on the farm. He needed a new job and different way to make money. He and his wife decided to move into town. They bought a small house in a nearby housing development, and Roger started his first-ever job search.

I asked Roger whether he felt like working at a car dealership was a big change from farming. He looked wistfully up the road, in the direction of his farm, then pointed to his big pickup truck and shrugged, saying, "at least I still have her."

Market Forces

Roger is one of the millions of workers projected to be displaced from their jobs because of technology. He is one of the lucky ones; he found another job in a different field. The World Economic Forum (WEF) predicts that just one in four adults who lose their jobs will be able to "upskill" and go on to compete in the job market. Listening to Roger and watching him tell his story, I felt the personal toll that comes when you realize you are no longer needed to do your job—for him, this was a loss of income and identity. There are practical, psychological, financial, and even spiritual implications to losing work or being underemployed.[7]

Being a dairy farmer provided Roger with an individual and community identity and it was where he derived much of his self-worth and pride. Who he was and how he made sense of the world tied back to being a dairy farmer. For him, this was dignified work. This is true for many professionals; as examples, consider the teachers, nurses, doctors, or small business owners you know.

In *The Job: Work and Its Future in a Time of Radical Change*, Ellen Ruppel Shell calls the combination of automation and globalization the "two-punch of job instability." Companies are in cutthroat competition against each other and the clock to offshore, outsource, and automate as much as

---

[7] David Blustein, *The Importance of Work in an Age of Uncertainty: The Eroding Work Experience in America* (Oxford University Press, 2019).

they can. In the world of online purchasing and same-day delivery (more characteristics of an Open Source Society), there is a demand for fast, cheap, and quality services and products.

While estimates vary, economists and futurists agree that somewhere around half of today's jobs will disappear or transform within the next decade. I predict it will be even more than that. I bet very few of these economists and futurists factored in global pandemics resulting in unprecedented job losses and economic recessions.

Changes in How We Work

In the future, our kids will compete for some jobs we recognize but many we do not. In the past decade, 94 percent of new jobs have been in nontraditional markets,[8] mostly temporary work. This accounts for a lot of gig economy work, including driving for Lyft and Uber, delivering food for GrubHub, or being a shopper for Instacart and Shipt. This also includes freelance and contract work. More people are independently employed, cobbling together several different jobs to get by.

Most of us know people who have combined their full-time job with gig or contract work in order to pay the bills. These include the pharmacist who delivers Instacart for me on the weekends, and the many Lyft and Uber drivers I have met who work evenings and weekends for supplemental pay. While there are real benefits to being your own boss and having flexibility over your schedule, many of these workers lack vital employment benefits and protections. Many end up working long hours, far exceeding typical 40-hour work weeks, and barely make ends meet.

Temporary Work and Gig Jobs

Holding down more than one job is something people have always done. What is new, is just how many people do it.[9] Roughly one-third of all

---

[8] Louis Hyman, *Temp: How American Work, American Business, and the American Dream Became Temporary* (Viking, 2018).
[9] Danny Vinik, "The Real Future of Work," *POLITICO*, 2018. https://www.politico.com/magazine/story/2018/01/04/future-work-independent-contractors-alternative-work-arrangements-216212.

working adults in the US engage in gig or temporary work.[10] In 2020, COVID-19 caused these numbers to seesaw dramatically.

Some gig positions—including package delivery and online shopping—increased in demand. These gigs were a fast and easy way for people to make quick money. However, many of these positions lacked basic worker protections and offered inadequate pay.

For freelance and contract workers, COVID-19 was particularly harmful. Many lost projects and hours. Others lost work contracts and clients entirely. For those out of work, many were unable to file for unemployment, given their independent status. Many couldn't access or afford healthcare coverage.

Even still, temporary work can help adults who are struggling with job or financial instability. People don't want to lose the jobs they have, even if the pay or hours aren't enough. By picking up odd jobs, they have an additional way to make up that income.

Most temporary work requires knowledge and skills that many adults already have. Most of us know how to grocery shop, drive a car, answer phones, or pick up and deliver a hot dinner. Thanks to Google Maps and Siri, there is little to learn, besides—perhaps—a new phone app. No need to go back to school or pay to get a new credential.

Different Types of Work

There are five different types of work[11] young people can expect to experience in adulthood, which may be done in person in workplace settings, remotely, or a mix of both:

- · **Full-Time Student.** This includes being in traditional degree programs at colleges and universities, as well as apprenticeships or new credentialing programs with non-traditional providers, such as bootcamps.

---

[10] Hyman, *Temp: How American Work, American Business, and the American Dream Became Temporary.*
[11] Thomas Ramge, Jan Schwochow, and Adrian Garcia-Landa, *The Global Economy As You've Never Seen It* (The Experiment Publishing, 2018).

- **Temporary Work.** This is on-demand work, including freelance and gig jobs. These workers are self-employed and only make money when they engage in service or product delivery. Some are part-time jobs for additional income or for fun; others are part-time jobs in a chosen occupation or career. Few of these jobs include critical benefits, such as healthcare.
- **Part-Time Work.** These are mostly retail, hospitality, and service work. This also includes workers in low-wage jobs caring for people. These workers include many home health aides, childcare workers, and teaching assistants.
- **Full-Time Work.** Once the pinnacle of stability, full-time workers may be salaried or self-employed. Salaried workers have set schedules, benefits, and employer protections. They can be unionized or at-will. Full-time workers can also be freelancers, consultants, and skilled workers in technical trades. Self-employed workers set their own hours and are responsible for their own benefits, including healthcare.
- **Civil Service, Service Corps, and Military.** These workers are employed by one of the branches of the US military or a public agency. Up until recently, many of these workers had strong job stability, a structured career ladder, and reliable pensions.

Over their working lives, today's kids will experience multiple types of work—in combination and rotation—and they will also engage in continuous learning throughout their careers. Those who live to old age will work more years than us, have more jobs, and probably experience multiple careers over many industries and sectors. With the growing prospect of a 100-year life, it is possible that many of today's kids could work for 70 years or more. As of now, our retirement systems and public safety nets are not designed to support people living and working that long (this includes social security, pensions, and retirement plans). This makes worker retirement and future financial stability increasingly uncertain.

Jobs of the Future

Today's kids are tomorrow's workers. As a workforce, they will operate in a market that is constantly changing and recreating itself. Workers will need to be able do the same. Big game changers, such as globalization and automation, will transform society and change the rules for how we work together, compete, use technology, and keep a job. Although today's recession-resilient young people want a reliable job and paycheck, it isn't promised.

Jobs on the Rise

In general, jobs that deal with advanced technology—sometimes referred to as "New Economy" work—will keep growing. Heard of Silicon Valley? Those tech tycoons near San Francisco will probably keep getting wealthier and more powerful, growing their companies and innovations, and holding their position as the twenty-first century Wall Street.

Machines will become more sophisticated and our kids will find that many jobs require working on and with those technologies or creating better options. The twentieth century worker was taught to act like machines. The early twenty-first century machines were taught to act like humans. Tomorrow's workers will need to be able to work with machines and act like themselves. There will be an enduring need for uniquely human skills.

In tomorrow's world, we will probably see the rise of the "Creative Class." Employers want workers who can think outside of the box, express curiosity, constantly learn, and who show a knack for problem-solving. As one person told me, "this is the wrong time in history to be ordinary." With AI working off of patterns and predictability, non-routine work will be our most durable work.

The Creative Class will be found working in full-time salaried positions and temp work, mostly freelance. For many creatives, work will be entrepreneurial and enabled by online technology platforms, such as Etsy or Square. It is likely that people will keep establishing virtual shops and be able to run a business without a building or staff.

Much of our future human work will live in education, care, community development, and service. Increasingly, these jobs are grouped together and referred to as the *care economy*. Having been in the care economy for my entire working life, I can attest to how very non-routine these jobs are. Robots might beat our world Jeopardy champions, but they have a long way to go before they can teach and manage a classroom of children, care for a group of toddlers, or meet the demands of adults with dementia. Inside of the care economy, we will see geriatrics and elder care grow in order to assist the needs of our large aging population.

JOBS THAT MAY ENDURE
· Teachers
· Nurses
· Chief executives
· Politicians

Jobs at Risk

Routine work is the riskiest work right now, and unfortunately, it is often the work of those who already struggle to get by. Many jobs of the twentieth century—the ones where humans work like machines—will not have homes as we get farther along in the twenty-first century.

Katherine Prince, a future forecaster at KnowledgeWorks, explained it to me this way: our job market is increasingly fragmented. Many people don't have a traditional job, but rather, spend their work hours completing tasks, projects, or short stints as contractors. As our employment structures get more and more fragmented, our work also becomes more subject to automation.

Consider executive assistants. Throughout the twentieth century, secretarial work provided many women and families the on-ramp they needed into the middle class. Today, these positions have largely disappeared. Most secretarial tasks can be accomplished with some combination of online email and calendaring programs, along with project management tools.

It is the same with factory workers. Go to any medium-sized city in the Rust Belt and you will find families who are scraping by on public support, whose worth and wealth were once proudly tied to factories that are either closed or operating with far fewer human workers. The automation of routine work is one of the greatest threats to our nation's working- and middle-classes.

JOBS THAT MAY DISAPPEAR
· Food preparers
· Cleaners
· Drivers
· Factory workers

Unforeseen Changes in the Workforce

There are some things we just can't predict about tomorrow's workforce, mostly because the market is tied to other factors, including the environment as well as our global relations and interdependencies. For instance, before COVID-19, hospitality, retail, and service work were considered durable work. Consumers were shopping and traveling, and these positions benefited from a uniquely human touch. And then a global pandemic stopped us from going out to shop, eat, or travel. Few outside of the infectious disease community would have predicted that this durable work would suddenly become so deeply distressed.

You Can't Be What You Can't See

As the workforce evolves and today's kids grow up, it is crucial for them to get exposure to and experience different types of work. Traditionally, we look to our families and communities to decide what kinds of jobs to pursue. My neighbor's son plays with trucks and tractors because his dad manages his family's truck company. I wanted to become a teacher because I was surrounded by them.

There is still value in this—and, as my mentor Greg Darnieder would say, "you can't be what you can't see." Exposure to and experience in emerging fields, through strong career pathways programming and work-based learning opportunities, is more important than ever. Increasingly, this needs to include work that can be done in an office or virtually and from a distance.

Helping Today's Kids Make It as Tomorrow's Workers

At the turn of the century, we were living and working in a knowledge economy. White-collared work, the kind that demanded critical thinking and academic credentials, was valued above blue-collared work, the jobs that required more manual labor and technical skills.

We are changing again. Now it is less about the color of your collar and more about whether you are in durable work, rather than work that is vulnerable to automation, outsourcing, or becoming obsolete. Some have said that even lawyers and doctors have jobs that are rote and patterned enough to one day be taken over by machines. Imagine a work world where suddenly the underappreciated but essential jobs of teaching and nursing are more valuable than prosecuting or prescribing medication.

We are transitioning into a learning economy, where relevancy and resiliency in the market is based on a worker's ability to continuously update and upgrade what they know and can do. Tomorrow's workers must be able to adapt to new and different situations. They cannot depend on a linear or singular career pathway that moves them from hire to retire, nor the guarantee that they will accrue status and wealth along the way. Instead, they need to be ready to work in one way and then pivot to something totally different. Beyond agility, this will require a degree of emotional fortitude, navigational and coping skills, and sufficient social supports.

Additionally, tomorrow's workers will need to be cognitively fit, showing up to work with solid executive functioning skills and the ability to pay attention in the midst of the distractions, overwhelm, and overload. No matter what job they have, tomorrow's workers will need to be able to concentrate and produce in an Open Source Society. This is not an easy task.

Along the way, tomorrow's workers will need to carry themselves through a number of professional transitions and transformations, taking on numerous career identities across their lifetimes of learning and work. In each time of change, they will do best if they can dig in and pull out the most vibrant and authentic versions of themselves, elevating their most distinctly human traits.

Life Currencies Needed for Tomorrow's World

For generations, the formula for economic success in the United States was widely accepted and enthusiastically endorsed: go to school, get good grades, graduate; earn a college degree, get a job that pays the bills, work hard, get promoted, and one day retire comfortably. That formula holds true for few people these days and even fewer in the future. We have seen how today's kids are changing and how the world is changing.

National experts, pundits, and politicians are sounding the alarm. The social contract of success in America does not work. The path of diploma-to-degree, college-to-career, then hire-to-retire no longer holds in a world where everything is changing.

Work is being so completely redefined that one day we may not recognize it. Gone are the days of becoming a "company man" or counting on a retirement with a pension.

What is the new formula for making it in America? It is time for us to update our widely held beliefs about what it means to ready for life.

Prepare for Tomorrow's Market, Not Yesterday's Assembly Line

For starters, let's acknowledge that the old formula was flawed from the start. It was designed to work best for those who are wealthy and white. And now it doesn't work for anyone. Graduating high school does not guarantee college. An Ivy League degree doesn't safeguard you from future job loss. And high test scores do not guarantee you have the skills needed for tomorrow's jobs.

The old formula for making it in adulthood was a completion checklist:

✓ Graduate high school and get a diploma.
✓ Graduate college and get a degree.
✓ Get a job.
✓ Get promoted or find a better job.
✓ Make money and manage responsibilities.
✓ Retire and live off your savings and investments.

The new formula for making it in adulthood is life currencies for the opportunity marketplace:

$ Continuously develop the *competencies* you need.
$ Pursue the *credentials* that prove to employers what you know and can do.
$ Form and nurture the *connections* to make it and move around.
$ Have enough *cash* to get by, get ahead, and smooth out.

Here is how this new opportunity marketplace works: imagine adult life as a series of transactions with various opportunity vendors. Each vendor requires certain currencies to access each opportunity—to purchase an experience you need the right amount of cash, competence, credibility, and connections. The currencies have different values and can be added up and offered in various combinations. As with any market, there are shoppers who have more than others, and there are people with so little that an opportunity vendor won't even consider selling to them.

Because of this, today's kids need to go well beyond content knowledge and passing grades. They will need to amass enough currency to afford the economic opportunities needed to make it into and through adulthood.

Currencies	Description
Competencies	The knowledge, skills, and abilities someone has
Connections	Who a person knows and is socially tied to
Credentials	The diploma, degrees, and certificates someone has
Cash	The financial resources someone has

Educators tend to focus on competencies and credentials. The classroom is where students acquire content knowledge and achieve academic standards. Although more educators are providing learning experiences that build social emotional skills along with content, doing so is often viewed as an add-on, or the practice of an exceptional teacher with some "secret sauce" for student engagement.

Having credentials and competencies is only part of what young people need to afford future opportunities, and continuing to focus on them to the exclusion of connections and cash—sometimes referred to as social and financial capital—will perpetuate inequity.

Opportunity Purchasing Power

In a market, it's all about having enough capital to get what you need. Purchasing power goes to those who have the most. Vendors aren't always fair, and they inflate prices and cut deals with people they know or who they perceive to be powerful.

Fair or not, without radical change this is how tomorrow's world will operate. There will be situations when just one or two currencies are needed, but more often than not, young people will need all four.

In the next part of the book, we unpack the currencies and consider strategies for helping young people learn and acquire them. Because currencies end up being spent, young people will need to know how and where to get more, otherwise they will run low or run out.

Currencies can be learned, earned, or inherited. Young people who are marginalized because of their identities or circumstances will need more currencies than others. The market is rigged, and it is unlikely that vendors will cut these young people a deal or give them preferential treatment.

Meanwhile, young people who are in the majority and who are socially and financially wealthy, will find more options available to them. Opportunities and privilege beget more opportunities and privilege. If we know more about what the currencies are and why they matter, then we can do more to make sure all young people enter adulthood with what they really need to succeed.

PART II

Life Currencies

CHAPTER 3

Competencies

competency: a specific range of skill, knowledge, or ability[1]

When I worked for the Forum for Youth Investment, my colleagues and I got funding to study the science (and art) of youth readiness. We dubbed our efforts *The Readiness Project*. For two years we dug deeply into the research, reading anything that clued us into what young people need for adulthood. Among other things, we considered what pediatricians look for, teachers test for, and employers demand. We compared the various authoritative lists of habits and skills—each deemed necessary for future success by whichever system or sector had issued it—and then tried to find what they all had in common. Eventually, we found a common set. We took that set and sifted it through the science of how young people learn and develop.

Ten Readiness Competencies

In the end, we published 10 universal readiness competencies. These were the bundles of knowledge, skills, and abilities most commonly used in life, learning, and work. These competencies operate as a set, building off each other. Think of these competencies as ways of being and doing in the world.

---

[1] Taken from *The American Heritage College Dictionary, 4th Edition*. 2002.

10 Competencies Today's Kids Need for Tomorrow's World

1. Focus and getting things done
2. Thinking and creating in ways that help to navigate, experience, and contribute to a rapidly changing world
3. Applying learning in the real world
4. Solving problems and making decisions
5. Getting and staying physically, emotionally, and cognitively fit
6. Feeling and expressing emotions appropriately
7. Persisting through struggles and maintaining hope
8. Relating to others and the world by forming, managing, and sustaining positive relationships
9. Being present and engaging in meaningful, authentic, and appropriate ways
10. Using insights to grow and develop

The best educators instinctively combine content delivery with competency development. Most of the time, they focus on the thinking competencies. The others get some attention, but they tend to be a byproduct of a positive learning environment or an engaging lesson.

Preparing kids for tomorrow's world requires us to focus on all 10 competencies. Every learning opportunity—inside or outside the classroom—should be viewed as a chance to learn, use, develop, or strengthen them.

For the past few years, a growing number of states and school districts have incorporated some of these competencies into their graduation requirements (numbers #2–4 on the list are most popular). While this is a great step forward, states and schools must understand that the only way young people can demonstrate those competencies is if the other six are working in the background.

Before we familiarize ourselves with these 10 competencies, here are a few things to keep in mind:

- **Every kid is wired differently.** Today's kids will acquire and require these competencies in their own ways. Those farthest behind or facing the most barriers will require the most.

- **Context and circumstances matter.** Different kids and situations require different amounts and combinations of the competencies.
- **These competencies do not reflect every skill and ability kids need.** There are plenty of important technical and academic skills that aren't on this list. These are just the universal ones they will use the most.
- **Most of these can be learned and developed early in life.** The earlier young people learn these and the more they practice, the better off they will be.

Focus and Get Things Done

Today's kids must learn to *focus and get things done*. This requires being able to concentrate and tune in, even amidst distractions. This also means being able to get and stay organized and having ways to manage a number of competing priorities and demands.

Throughout their lives, today's kids will need to work hard to focus and accomplish things. The continuous onslaught of information, options, and notifications will constantly vie for their time and attention. Digital distractions will abound. Focus, concentration, and task completion will be increasingly difficult.

To focus and get things done in the future, today's kids need to learn how to:

- Follow and remember instructions.
- Manage distractions.
- Be mindful and present.
- Get and stay organized.
- Complete tasks and projects.
- Practice self-awareness.
- Build a growth mindset.
- Communicate needs.
- Turn digital devices on and off, at-will.

Cal Newport learned a lot about this competency while researching his books, *Deep Work* and *Digital Minimalism*. From that research and his own experience, he believes "the ability to focus without distraction" is essential for future survival. Cal describes concentration as an increasingly rare commodity, one that improves its worth with practice.

One of the greatest threats to this competency is the device ding. Those pesky notifications disrupt whatever you are doing to tell you something you usually don't need to know in that moment. Each notification acts as a digital drug or slot machine, sending a rush of pleasure chemicals through the body and brain. Getting notifications or refreshing a page to check how many people have liked something you've posted, creates a biological response similar to getting high. So, if you feel like you or your kids are addicted to devices—it might be more than a feeling.

Beyond devices, there are other distractions that make it hard for kids to focus or get things done. Fears, anxieties, and worry can draw a different response from the brain. When stress or fears go up, adrenaline kicks in and draws thoughts and attention to whatever is causing angst. This fight, flight, or freeze mode can make it feel impossible to concentrate on anything else.

Imagine you were expecting a phone call from your doctor to discuss important test results. Would you be able to concentrate on work tasks? Probably not unless you had specific concentration and mindfulness techniques to put in play.

To withstand the avalanche of distractions and disruptions, today's kids need ways to calm down, refocus, get quiet, and tune in. This takes time and tools, as well as practice.

How to Build This Competency

There are some hacks to use while developing longer-term strategies. These include using noise-canceling headphones while doing work in loud spaces, turning off device notifications, shutting down the "gallery view" on Zoom, or using apps that block certain websites. There are apps that do this; they have names that reflect the issue at hand: Freedom, BrainFocus, BreakFree, just to name a few.

Kids will need to learn how to focus and get things done while digitally connected and while unplugged. Being able to shift from in-person to online is more important than ever.

Strengthening executive functioning is a great way to activate this competency. Executive functioning is the part of our brain that helps us organize, remember, and process information. It also helps us exercise self-control—super important when tempted to keep clicking on YouTube videos instead of completing assignments.

WAYS TO PRACTICE FOCUSING AND GETTING THINGS DONE

- Puzzles
- Board games
- Memory games
- Listening to a concert, or watching a movie or sports game from start to finish
- Keeping a calendar, planner, or organizer
- Mindfulness exercises

Think, Create, and Apply

Today's kids must learn to *think and create* in ways that enable them to navigate, experience, and contribute to a rapidly changing world. They have to be able to *apply their ideas and know-how* to real-world situations to solve complex tasks and problems.

Tomorrow's world will require tremendous creativity and innovation. The newness and risk of emergent challenges will require critical thinking and discernment. Adults will be lifetime learners and workers, so learning, thinking, and applying need to become lifelong practices.

To think, create, and apply in the future, today's kids need to learn how to:

- Use their imagination.
- Be flexible, being able to shift from one thing to another.
- Learn how to learn.
- Be strategic.
- Be open-minded.
- Remain curious and reflective.
- Try new things.
- Take healthy risks.
- Persist when things don't go as planned.

How to Build These Competencies

There are some great ways to develop and strengthen this competency. Consider STEAM activities or MakerSpace programs set up in school or at home. A couple years ago, I took the boys to our school district's daylong MakerSpace camp. Within two hours, my boys had programmed robots to roll around the gymnasium floor; they had created an imaginary world with physical blocks that converted into a virtual video game; and—their personal favorite—they built different LEGO structures that got plugged in and animated by code. My older son built a helicopter that released a ladder to save a LEGO panda. My younger son built a truck that zoomed from one end of the table to the other, complete with flashing sirens.[2]

Consider these five MakerSpace rules that were taped on the wall in bright colors:

1. **Ask.** Define the problem. What are the challenges?
2. **Imagine.** Brainstorm ideas. Pick the best one.
3. **Plan.** Make a model or draw a diagram. Gather materials.
4. **Create.** Test the model. Follow the plan.
5. **Improve.** Did it work? How can you make it better? Repeat steps 1-4 to make changes.

These rules capture what kids need to be good thinkers and tinkerers. They are also excellent guideposts for any learning project or assignment.

In the future, most of us will feel like we are constant newbies, always trying to understand what's happening and then trying to make sense of it.[3] Tomorrow's forces—machines, momentum, and market changes—will require that young people be able to think for themselves and apply what they know to a lesser-known landscape. This level of creative thinking will require perseverance and a confidence to take risks and try new things.[4]

---

[2] LEGO now makes different versions designed for use at home or school.
[3] Kevin Kelly, *The Inevitable: Understanding the 12 Technological Forces That Will Shape Our Future* (Penguin Books, 2016).
[4] Scott Barry Kaufman and Carolyn Gregoire, *Wired to Create: Unraveling the Mysteries of the Creative Mind* (Perigree, 2015).

Strange as it may seem, another way to strengthen this competency is to help kids learn to manage their stress, reduce anxiety, and get enough sleep and healthy food. Being stressed, tired, or hungry can pull energy away from the "thinking" and "applying" part of the brain—the executive in the front—and send it to the back—the amygdala, which is the more primitive part of our brain. When that happens, kids go into survival mode and the urge to fight or flee overrides the ability to think and create. When we are trying to survive, our mental energy belongs to our muscles, limbs, eyesight, and senses.[5]

Lastly, researchers have found a direct link between this competency and being able to focus and get things done. This link reinforces that in order for today's kids to be good thinkers and creators, they must also work on the other nine competencies.

WAYS TO APPLY LEARNING AND
PRACTICE CRITICAL AND CREATIVE THINKING

- Simulations, improv, and acting
- Creative writing
- Games that foster critical and creative thinking
- Coding apps and games
- Idle time

Solve Problems and Make Decisions

Today's kids must learn to *solve problems and make decisions*. This requires the ability to look at a situation or scenario, familiarize yourself with it, and then figure out what needs to be done. Solving problems and making decisions go hand in hand. They should be viewed as an ongoing process rather than something to accomplish.

---

[5] Kids who are in toxic environments, facing hardship or experiencing trauma might find themselves constantly struggling to think and learn because they are biologically on high alert. Experiencing racism and oppression is a form of everyday toxic stress, and it takes a toll on a young person's sense of self, and their ability to learn and develop. Brain scans show that kids who experience chronic stress and trauma develop an enlarged amygdala and an immature prefrontal cortex (which means their executive functioning skills end up underdeveloped). Basic gardening principles apply: what you water will grow. The prefrontal cortex develops all the way through early adulthood. It is super sensitive and malleable during early childhood and again in adolescence (ages 10 to 26). If you want to give kids the chance to be great thinkers and creators, you have to help them manage stress, deal with trauma, and stay calm.

Tomorrow's world will include predictable problems and novel ones. We will face new global and political challenges, some of which seem far off and improbable today. In the workplace, today's kids will lead, manage, and respond to entirely new relationships with technology, the environment, security—even outer space. This will bring up new moral and ethical questions, and opportunities to innovate.

To solve problems and make decisions in the future, today's kids need to learn how to:

- Be a good planner.
- Be resourceful.
- Think critically and creatively.
- Communicate and listen well.
- Manage conflict.
- Know when to deliberate and when to take action.
- Be practical.
- Cultivate empathy and compassion.

How to Build This Competency

Play is an important part of developing and strengthening this competency. Beginning in early childhood, kids use play to learn how to communicate, negotiate, problem solve, and make decisions. This happens in group settings—at recess or during group activities—and on their own. With younger kids, you can watch a child activate this competency when he converts a cardboard box into a rocket ship, or a bin of stuffed animals into an epic birthday party. With older ones, you can see this in the art and music they create, the stories they tell, or the team challenges they solve.

Two of my favorite authors, brothers Chip and Dan Heath, discuss the art of problem-solving and decision-making in their book *Decisive*. In the book, they talk about how important it is to weigh various options and consider others' perspectives before making a decision. The things that tend to get in the way of good problem-solving and decision-making include narrow thinking, acting emotionally, short-sightedness, and seeking out confirmation that you're right. Today's kids could be more susceptible to these pitfalls because they will be solving problems and making decisions in a fast, frantic world.

I spoke about this with Paul Gaffney, chief technology officer at Kohl's. He pointed out that new solutions and products available all the time means that today's kids need ways to compare and evaluate options and then decide what is best. Their problem-solving and decision-making will need to be quick, continuous, and reflexive. It will help if they can develop strong resource management, cognitive flexibility, and emotional strength.

Imagine spending lots of time solving a complicated problem, only to have it resurface a few months later. We have all experienced this, and so will today's kids—just more often. Paul stressed that they will need to know where to go to see if problems have changed and what to do when that happens. Doing that will activate the other competencies, especially focus, persistence, and creativity.

Ways to Practice Problem-Solving and Decision-Making

- Cooking or building something
- Simulations and improv
- Debates and opinion writing
- Scavenger hunts and puzzles
- Play, including games and organized activities
- Teaching others (e.g., being a peer leader or "buddy" to someone younger)

Get and Stay Fit

Today's kids must learn to *get and stay physically, emotionally, and cognitively fit*. Personal health is necessary to live, learn, and work. Personal health is also hard to maintain if you live in poverty or are in crisis. In addition to individual health practices, young people need access to quality and affordable healthcare, including behavioral health services.

Our current realities and the unknown future will stretch today's kids to the max and their health will directly impact their ability to show up to school and perform on the job. Education exercises the mind, and the mind is part of the body. Kids' health directly affects how they learn and develop.

Tomorrow's world will come with new and different health risks. Everything from water and infrastructure issues, to superbugs and megacities.

Information and digital distractions will overwhelm and overload. Through it all, today's kids will need ways to stay healthy and cognitively fit.

To get and stay fit in the future, today's kids must learn how to:

- Strengthen executive functioning skills.
- Practice self-care, especially physical fitness and relaxation techniques.
- Activate basic life management skills.
- Be resourceful.
- Practice self-awareness.
- Cultivate a degree of hope and optimism.
- Manage screen time, being able to connect and disconnect at will.
- Maintain positive connections with others.
- Cope with hardship.

I witnessed the connection between health and education every day at the school I ran for overage and undercredited youth. Our school served young people who were fighting for the chance to finish high school. They had been previously pushed or pulled out of school because of life challenges. The odds were stacked against them. Many juggled school with part-time jobs, a number were parents, and almost all lived in poverty. Neighborhood violence was common, and each had stories of personal tragedies and trauma.

We did what we could to support them. We had social workers and solid case management services. We partnered with every community agency we could find. At school, students could connect to medical and psychiatric services, counseling and housing, food banks, and childcare. Supporting their health with community services and supports paid off. Once supports were in place, we watched students who were falling behind or disappearing from our roster, suddenly show up and engage.

This is a competency we can easily track in our own lives. Looking back, I can point to times when my physical or mental health made learning or working easier or more difficult. On a daily basis, I know how much harder it is to show up and meet my obligations when I am tired, worried, or hungry. On the other hand, I feel like anything is possible when I am regularly exercising and feel centered and content.

How to Build This Competency

To understand the components of this competency, consider fitness and health across four dimensions:

1. **Physical.** Today's kids need access to healthy food to nourish their brains and bodies. They need enough sleep to focus and think when they're awake.[6] If they have a health condition, their symptoms and medications need to be well-managed.

2. **Emotional.** Kids need to feel safe and supported. Most days, they should feel calm and in control, free from harmful thoughts or actions. If they have a mental health condition, their symptoms and medications need to be well-managed.

3. **Cognitive.** Kids should always be working to strengthen and develop their executive functioning skills, which won't be fully formed until their mid-twenties. They should have practices that help them calm down, concentrate, and get centered when they face unknowns, uncertainty, or are feeling overloaded and overwhelmed. Cognitive fitness includes being able to self-regulate, focus, organize, remember things, be flexible, pay attention, and complete tasks. For kids with cognitive differences, this will require additional tools and supports.

4. **Social.** Kids should know who to connect with, and when. They should have people and organizations to turn to for support and enjoyment. They should have spaces and peer groups where they feel loved and that they belong, along with strategies to engage in positive and healthy ways.

---

[6] Kids need sleep, but rarely get enough. I once met a woman in Ohio who was campaigning to change high school start times. She was gravely concerned about how early high school started, and how it affected teens' safety, learning, and development. She exposed me to irrefutable evidence that older youths' internal biological clocks are set for them to fall asleep around 11 P.M. or 12 A.M. and wake up around 10 A.M. or 11 A.M. the next morning. Older youth need more sleep than adults and late nights or hard-to-rouse mornings are not defiance but legitimate exhaustion and biological wiring. Today's kids get an hour less sleep each night than 30 years ago. This sleep would help them to learn and remember things, and better manage their emotions.

These health and fitness dimensions set a minimum bar for what kids need to make it in the future. This competency stretches far beyond classrooms and into our homes and communities. Fitness demands access to nutritious food, preventative healthcare, and mental health supports. Life disrupters, such as hunger and homelessness, trauma, or a mental health crisis, are things that can and do happen; but they should be temporary and recoverable. This is a foundational competency that requires immediate intervention if it is not well developed.

WAYS TO PRACTICE GETTING AND STAYING FIT

- Routine wellness visits with quality healthcare providers
- Exercise and recreation
- Playing on a sports team
- Spending time in nature
- Cooking and eating with others
- Letter writing or keeping a journal
- Having a hobby or joining a club
- Getting enough sleep—including naps if necessary

Respond, Regulate, and Persist

Today's kids must learn to *feel and express emotions appropriately.* As they experience changes and challenges, they must have what it takes to *persist, maintain hope, and use insights to grow and develop.*

Tomorrow's world will include a number of transitions and transformations. Some sudden and unexpected, others anticipated and prepared for. Whether good or bad, these times will always be disruptive and bring stress. With kids living longer, they need reliable strategies for making sense of struggles; this will enable them to keep going and growing, even when times are tough. This includes healthy coping skills, sufficient self-regulation, and the ability to find meaning and acceptance when unexplainably hard things happen. This competency does best in healthy, positive relationship with others.[7]

---

[7] Linda Gratton and Andrew Scott, *The 100-Year Life: Living and Working in an Age of Longevity* (Bloomsbury, 2017).

In addition to coping with the tougher stages and phases of life, today's kids will need healthy ways to engage in virtual spaces and with technology. A digital world is more exposed and often has less privacy. It opens young people up to the risks of cyberbullying and anonymous criticism or distant cruelty. It is a world defined by hyperconnectivity, consumption, immediacy, and access.[8] Online, our lives are increasingly public and documented, which brings new concerns about how to respond, regulate, and reflect when something happens.

To respond, regulate, and persist in the future, today's kids must learn how to:

- Practice self-care and self-awareness.
- Control impulses and manage emotions.
- Strengthen cognitive flexibility.
- Establish positive connections and relationships with others.
- Maintain an open mind.
- Cultivate compassion and empathy.
- Be mindful and reflective.

Many of today's kids are already having a hard time with this competency. The stress of life is getting them sick and inflaming mental health issues, especially anxiety and depression. Every time I talk about this book, people tell me how worried they are about the mental health of young people.

One university administrator told me his university can't keep up with students' mental health needs. Every year, more students attempt suicide. Anxiety is at an all-time high, and some students are taking medical leaves and going home. A former professor has had the same experience. Every semester, more students drop out midway through his course because they can't manage their anxiety or depression along with college demands. Another professor explained it this way: "Too many students are immobilized by their mental health issues, and ultimately they are being brought down by their fear, anxiety, and sadness."

This isn't just college students. We have a family member who is a school psychologist. In the past few years, she has had to conduct

---

[8] Kevin Kelly, *The Inevitable: Understanding the 12 Technological Forces That Will Shape Our Future* (Penguin Books, 2016).

two or more suicide assessments each week, sometimes for kids as young as eight!

Why are today's kids having such a hard time? Reasons run the gamut. Maybe it's too much technology or cyberbullying; scarier environmental conditions, discrimination, and family stressors; fear of or response to school shootings, pandemics, and natural disasters; unrealistically high expectations for academic performance; even just knowing that life could be long and hard.

In a perfect world, our colleges and schools would have the budgets for the counseling supports and mental health services today's kids need. This probably will not happen.

To figure out what to do without those supports in place, I turned to my colleague, Cristal McGill. Cristal is my go-to expert on all things education psychology, neuroscience, and student resiliency. Cristal has worked in schools across the US—from large urban districts, to residential facilities in the most remote parts of Alaska. In her experience, fostering resilience is the key to helping kids respond, regulate, and persist. Young people need to learn how to bounce back from tough times; find control and purpose; and bring order to chaos.

How to Build These Competencies

Here are some strategies kids can practice to build resiliency.[9] Resiliency will enable them to better respond to situations and—as research shows—subsequently calm down and combat the rising tide of stress, anxiety, and depression:

- Learn how to focus on the present.
- Practice downtime.
- Learn to harness an inner strength during challenging times.
- Stay open to new possibilities.
- Reach out to friends and family for support.
- Practice gratitude.
- Connect to a bigger purpose, spiritually or otherwise.
- Find meaning in failures or mistakes.

---

[9]Jim Rendon, *Upside: The New Science of Post-Traumatic Growth* (Touchstone, 2015).

- Learn to apologize when wrong and seek to repair damaged relationships.

Cristal sees safe and supportive learning environments as the perfect places to practice these strategies. By learning and practicing them throughout childhood and adolescence, these strategies can become strong and reliable enough to keep using throughout adulthood.

WAYS TO PRACTICE RESPONDING, REGULATING, AND PERSISTING

- Role playing
- Morning meetings or other forms of checking in
- Restorative and healing-centered practices
- Creative writing or keeping a journal
- Social emotional skill development

Relate and Engage with Others

Today's kids must learn to *relate to others and the world* by forming, nurturing, and *sustaining healthy relationships*. They must know how to be present with others, engaging them in appropriate, authentic, and meaningful ways.

Today's kids will have a lifetime of engaging in-person and online. Longer lives will lead to more relationships and longer stints of parenting and partnering. Lifetime friendships will become increasingly important.[10]

Beyond human relationships, young people will need to figure out how to emotionally engage with machines, especially artificial intelligence. Today's kids may actually be faced with future decisions like whether they want a robot for a co-worker, or as their children's nurse or nanny. These science fiction storylines will become a part of everyday life.

---

[10] Julia Hobsbawm, *Fully Connected: Social Health in an Age of Overload* (Bloomsbury, 2018).

Today's kids are also growing up in a more diverse and crowded world. It will be necessary to learn how to respect personal differences and cultures. In an Open Source Society there will be more globalization and connectivity, especially through digital mediums. Being able to relate and engage will be foundational, and the associated behaviors and habits should start to be learned and practiced in childhood.

To relate and engage with others in the future, today's kids must learn how to:

- Practice self-control and self-awareness.
- Communicate and listen well.
- Know who and what to connect with and when.
- Manage and maintain relationships.
- Cope with hardship and uncertainty.
- Practice diplomacy and conflict management.
- Be adaptable.
- Stay open-minded and curious.
- Cultivate compassion and empathy.
- Pay attention and be present.

This competency will be especially important in tomorrow's workforce. Work will run on a reimagined relationship between humans and machines. Everyone will be in touch-tech relationships that require active engagement with and in technology.[11] Employment will fluctuate. When jobs are secure, we will enjoy our relationships with co-workers. When jobs are unstable or lost, we will need support from our family and friends.

How to Build These Competencies

Learning to relate and engage with others—especially those who are different than we are—happens through exposure and experience. I saw this in action when I visited the 2019 Illinois Teacher of the Year, Susan Converse, in her "Tiger Den" at Edwardsville High School. Susan is a

---

[11] Paul R. Daugherty and James H Wilson, *Human + Machine: Reimagining Work in the Age of AI* (Harvard Business Review Press, 2018).

special education teacher who started a student-run cafe. At the Tiger Den, students with special needs—ranging from high-functioning autism, to severe developmental delays and physical limitations—pair with general education students to cook, bake, and sell hot drinks and pastries.

This learn-and-work model places *neurodivergent* young people—that is, those who are neurologically or developmentally different than the norm—next to *neurotypical* young people. In the cafe setting, they are able to work together to deliver a valuable service to the broader school community. The benefits are numerous and build more than competencies, but the other currencies as well—cash, connections, and credit toward a credential. Through the Tiger Den experience, young people get the real-time training they need to live and work with people who are different than they are.

WAYS TO PRACTICE RELATING AND ENGAGING

- Group activities and projects
- Youth-led forums and ventures
- Internships
- Organized sports and clubs
- Free play, recreation, and recess
- Volunteering
- Peer mentoring or buddy programs

Competencies in Context

Now that we know more about the 10 most commonly used readiness competencies, let's consider context. It matters a lot. In the same way that we have body systems that keep us physically alive (e.g., cardiovascular, muscular) we have competency systems that enable us to function in the world.

Competencies by Age, Stage, and Situation

The competencies look different, depending on how old kids are, who they are, where they are developmentally, and what they are trying to do. In spite of the fact that we organize most youth experiences by age or grade, it doesn't always match where they are or what they need. As we know, kids develop on their own unique timetables.

Consider the growth charts pediatricians use to track height and weight. We should have similar ones for young people's cognitive, social, and emotional development. There's a range of what is typical, and then there is a trajectory for what is projected or needed for each individual young person.

Here's why age and stage matters: it would be unrealistic to expect young children to focus and get things done, uninterrupted, for longer then—let's say—10 minutes. It would be even harder for those with ADHD behaviors, especially if they are being asked to do something they don't want to do. The basic rule with focus is that kids can do it for as many minutes as they are years old. It caps at 20 minutes. That means it is perfectly normal for a developmentally typical five-year-old to get distracted after five minutes of doing an activity.

Now consider context. We apply the general rule, and then adjust it depending on who the kid is and what is happening. For young people with attention or spectrum disorders, I might shave off how many minutes I expect them to focus—unless they are doing something they love, in which case I might add more time. When kids are hungry, I take time away—same thing if they are distracted. And so on.

Competencies at the Margins

Many young people have to work much harder than others to make it. Every day they take on challenges that are invisible to the majority. This is because society and systems of care (schools, hospitals, etc.) were designed for society's most privileged: those who are wealthy, white, and able-bodied. Anyone who doesn't meet those criteria cannot be optimally served.

This means that in every community, school, and program, there are kids whose race, ethnicity, religion, gender or sexual identity, legal status, financial situation, home life, and/or physical and mental health realities force them to work harder than others, by no fault of their own. Operating from the margins takes additional skill and strategy to navigate everyday realities and expectations.

Systems expect kids to perform equally even when some are fighting against unasked for struggle, stereotype, and stigma. Without massive societal and systems change, this will be something they face for the rest of their lives.

We must keep an open mind and keen perception, getting to know the young people in our lives and learning their histories and realities. Doing this will enable us to better assist them in developing the competencies they most need, in the ways they need them.

Competencies and the Other Currencies

Competencies are highly interdependent with the other currencies that kids need to make it—cash, connections, and credentials. To be competent but not financially or socially situated is like trying to draw a bath without a stopper in the drain. It makes everything harder, and sometimes impossible. The less cash and healthy connections kids have, the harder it will be to develop and strengthen their competencies. It is easier for a young person to "get and stay fit" or "think and create" when their needs are met, their bellies are full, and their minds are rested.

The amount of cash, connections, and credentials someone has will either power or deplete the competencies. As we consider what today's kids need for tomorrow's world, we need to understand that the competencies work together and with the other currencies. We cannot expect young people to make it in life if they are competent enough, but still lack basic resources, supports, and qualifications.

CHAPTER 4

Connections

connections: *who you know and who knows you*

When I was 16, I left New Jersey and moved to South Florida to start college. I took my framed GED, a few suitcases, a skateboard, and gumption. I was leaving a small town where everybody knew me, for a place where I didn't know anyone. New Jersey was where I made lifetime friendships rooted in a shared childhood. It was also a place where adults broadcast doubts on what I could do with my life. To launch, I needed to leave.

In Florida, my social circle grew with purpose and possibility. Besides being in college, I was in early recovery. I went to Alcoholics Anonymous (AA) meetings every day, and because I was too young to drive, all of my meetings needed to be in walking distance. Those meetings happened to be on Palm Beach island.

Palm Beach is the wealthiest community in the United States. It is otherworldly with its perfectly manicured lawns, beautiful mansions, clean streets, and straight rows of palm trees. The island is a mile wide and a few miles long. It is famous for wealthy site-seeing and a shopping strip aptly named Worth Avenue.

At night, I would walk across the intracoastal from my West Palm Beach dorm room to AA meetings held in island churches and restaurants. For an hour, I would sit with a group of people whose social status and worth exceeded anything I had ever experienced myself.

Those hours and fellow alcoholics deeply influenced who I am today. Recovery acted as a bridge into a different social class from the one I grew up in. Over time, I learned the behaviors and conversation patterns of America's elite. Technically, I was still in the prime of adolescence, which made these experiences particularly formative. Between my wealthy recovering friends and college classmates, I learned new ways of approaching life and navigating challenges. I became comfortable in a new social stratosphere, all while still benefiting from the gifts of my hometown friendships.

My college years remain some of the best years of my life. With the nudging and nurturing of a remarkable social network, my possible future evolved and expanded. By staying rooted in recovery principles and community, I was able to grow and aspire to a life beyond anything I had previously hoped for.

Wired to Connect

We are wired for community and connection. We need each other, by design. Our bodies and brains respond in positive, powerful ways when we are with the people we care about. The quality of these relationships effects who we are, how we behave, the choices we make, and how long we live.[1] With many of today's kids on track to live 100 years or more, these connections are more important than ever.[2]

As they grow up, young people will need people surrounding and supporting them through tremendous change and personal transition. These connections will need to go beyond the surface level. Digital social network platforms will be a core part of how kids connect but will never be as powerful as the real thing. We should look to these forms of digital communication as great tools for staying in touch with people and expanding social horizons, but also understand that it rarely has the same nourishing quality as face-to-face interactions.[3]

Instead, encourage young people to view these platforms as an interactive directory of social connections, a great place to store and

---

[1] Susan Pinker, *The Village Effect: Why Face-to-Face Contact Matters*. 2nd ed. (Atlantic Books, 2015).
[2] Gratton and Scott, *The 100-Year Life: Living and Working in an Age of Longevity* (Bloomsbury Business, 2017).
[3] Pinker, *The Village Effect: Why Face-to-Face Contact Matters*. 2nd ed.

maintain a large repository of the people we are connected to. My college experience was exceptional because of my ability to engage in real life with people on campus and on the island. My long-distance connections—which were limited at the time to phone calls—were important touchpoints, but not sufficient on their own. Today, I am still connected with many of these people from my past via social network platforms, while relying more on the immediate and in-person support I receive from the people I live and work with.

Today's kids are hyperconnected, and yet, seem to feel increasingly alone and isolated. This only became heightened when COVID-19 forced us all into varying levels of physical isolation. Social networks broadcast hundreds or thousands of "friends" and likes, all while people report fewer friends and loved ones to turn to during tough times. This is really bad news, especially because times are increasingly difficult.

My colleague Jaime-Alexis Fowler, founder of Empower Work—a digital platform that helps workers navigate complicated employment situations—thinks about this as a form of cognitive dissonance. The volume of kids' digital connections has led to a kind of social fatigue. Both adults and kids post about their lives to their social network of "friends," but would invite only a few to dinner, or ask only a couple for help if they needed it, even for something as small as a ride home.

Connections That Matter Most

The social lives of today's kids must extend far beyond digital "friends" and shallow forms of hyperconnectivity. In a strange and unpredictable world, today's kids need a vibrant, diverse, and durable assembly of friends, supports, and social connections. Most of all, they need *lifelines, door openers,* and *navigators.* These individuals form the base of a young person's social network—the kind that extends beyond social media—to provide real life care, community, identity, opportunity, and power.

- **Lifelines.** *Lifelines* are the people who have your back, no matter what. Their role is to cheer you on, pick you up, and push you forward when life is hard. Lifelines can be friends, co-workers, mentors, clergy, counselors, teachers, coaches, or family members. They offer safety, stability, and support. These are the people who you care for and who care for you. Lifelines do not need to increase a young person's social capital. They just need to be there, meeting the young person where they are, offering free and ongoing love and support.

- **Door Openers.** *Door openers* do not need to be in your life for long. A door opener might be a lifeline (or become one later) but doesn't have to be. This is a person who or program that opens the door to a better opportunity, perhaps one that might have been closed or otherwise unknown. Door openers are social mobilizers and bridges, introducing or integrating young people into their own networks and groups, extending their social capital and connections to provide new social, cultural, and economic benefits. Those born into wealthy families may inherit powerful door openers. Not having access to door openers inflames disparities.

- **Navigators.** *Navigators* are people who help us figure out how a new opportunity, environment, or experience works. Navigators can be counselors, mentors, supervisors, or peer advisors. They can be self-appointed or assigned. In school, navigators might be someone older, like a student leader with a similar background, or even a caring teacher or professor. In the workplace, navigators can be colleagues from the same department or location who have been there longer. Navigators may have had a similar experience with a system or situation—sometimes because they share an identity with the young person, such as race or gender. Navigators help us understand the culture of a place, what to expect and what is expected of us. Navigators might start off as door openers and can often become lifelines, but that is not always the case. Navigators are the people to ask what something means, where something is, or how to get something done.

The research on the power of these types of relationships is clear. Positive social connections and capital will help today's kids to learn more, work harder, and live longer.[4]

---

[4] Julia Hobsbawm, *Fully Connected: Social Health in an Age of Overload* (Bloomsbury, 2018).

Lifelines

I would not be who I am if not for the guys at Vito's Pizza, Mrs. Lewis, Lindsay, Dr. Poe, Ali, Barbara, Amanda, Gautam, and Jim. These mentors, along with my parents, were lifelines through my teen years and into early adulthood. I relied on them for ongoing guidance that was free from judgment but full of accountability and good advice. Each featured in a different season of life, and all supported me in every area of life. For me, it wasn't one caring adult who helped me along the way, but many.

I would not be here if not for my dearest friends, who I refer to as my "lifers." These are the friends who I have journeyed with through loss and struggle, celebrations and milestones.

Lifelines are young people's social and emotional superglue. They provide unending amounts of belonging, solidarity, acceptance, and meaning.[5] These are the people who stand by and show up, in good times and bad. They offer love without expectation, and even when distance or time separates, they feel like coming "home" after a separation. Lifeline relationships are born out of mutual respect and shared experience. I love and trust my lifelines, and I know they feel the same way about me. These are not transactional relationships used to get ahead; they are relationships built on mutual respect, enjoyment, care, and commitment.

Tomorrow's unknowns and risks will warrant strong lifelines. This is especially true for a generation of young people who crave stability, security, and constancy. In a time when that is not possible environmentally, it can be possible socially. Throughout life, these longings can be filled by friendships, mentorships, and family relationships.

Links between Lifelines, Learning, and Work

If today's kids have strong and positive social supports they will be far more likely to stay in school[6] and get and find the work they need.[7] If you

---

[5] Sam M. Intrator and Don Siegel, *The Quest for Mastery: Positive Youth Development Through Out-of-School Programs* (Harvard Education Press, 2014).
[6] Julia Freeland Fisher and Daniel Fisher, *Who You Know: Unlocking Innovations That Expand Students' Networks* (Jossey-Bass, 2018).
[7] Llana Gershon, *Down and Out in the New Economy: How People Find (or Don't Find) Work Today* (University of Chicago Press, 2017).

want to know if kids will go to college or get a good job, just look to see if their friends are doing it, or if the adults in their life are pushing them toward it. The behaviors of those closest to us are biologically contagious.[8] We tend to do what our friends and family do, and for those who don't, it takes effort. This is because we pay attention to the things that people, we care about, care about.

Beyond social contagion, how we learn and work corresponds to how we are doing socially and emotionally. This is especially true for young people; that's because social and emotional experiences are more important and intense in adolescence than other times in life.[9]

It is really hard to focus at school or on the job if you have social anxiety, feel excluded, or are fighting with friends and family. Teachers and youth workers see this all the time. This is one reason why having an inclusive and positive learning environment is so important. Experience tells us that if a young person feels they don't belong, their performance and behavior will suffer. Experience also tells us that kids flourish, work harder, and perform better when they are in places with positive and responsive cultures, surrounded by people who care.

As I learned from Boston College professor, David Blustein, this stays true as we get older. David is a psychologist who studies work relationships and the future of work. In addition to teaching, he has been a clinician most of his career, mostly focused on helping adults through periods of unemployment, work transitions, as well as other issues. David told me that adults rely on work for many of their social connections and contributions. He sees work as a critical way people connect with the pulses of the world.[10] I can relate. As adults, we spend more time on the

---

[8] Nicholas A. Christakis and James H. Fowler, *Connected: The Surprising Power of Our Social Networks and How They Shape Our Lives* (Little, Brown and Company, 2009).

[9] Committee on the Neurobiological and Socio-behavioral Science of Adolescent Development and Its Applications, Board on Children, Youth, and Families, Division of Behavioral and Social Sciences and Education, Health and Medicine Division, and National Academies of Sciences, Engineering, and Medicine. *The Promise of Adolescence: Realizing Opportunity for All Youth.* Edited by Richard J. Bonnie and Emily P. Backes (Washington, DC: National Academies Press, 2019). https://doi.org/10.17226/25388.

[10] Emilie Le Beau Lucchesi, "The Stresses of the Way We Work Now," *The New York Times*, May 14, 2020, https://www.nytimes.com/2020/05/14/well/mind/coronavirus-work-stress-unemployment-depression-anxiety.html.

job with co-workers, than with our families.[11] Many of us count on our colleague conversations and work friendships to satisfy social needs—much the same way children look forward to going to school so they can see their classmates.

The nature and structure of work will look different in tomorrow's world—more transient, remote, and disparate. Workers will be more likely to connect virtually and work for themselves or multiple organizations. They will change jobs and job locations more often—and so will their colleagues. These changing dynamics may make it harder to create and retain deep and meaningful professional friendships. This makes lifelines outside of work more vital—particularly during times of unemployment or job transition.

Lifelines over a Lifetime

Imagine living to be 100, or older. The quality of your life—as demographers and scientists have discovered—will be determined, in large part, by the vibrancy of your social network and supports.[12] As social animals, our bodies and brains correspond to how we are doing relationally. For instance, there are numerous reports of women being far more likely to beat cancer if they have a tight web of social supports throughout treatment; those who go the road alone, are more likely to stay sick or even pass away. Scientists have proven that positive social interactions can boost immunity and productivity. Experience tells us that we just feel better and do better when we know there are people around us who have our backs.

When lifelines organize around a person or cause, it generates a level of strength and power that goes well beyond what any individual can offer. These groups can mobilize to produce social power critical for producing large-scale change; this lifeline group power is a building block

---

[11] Ellen Ruppel Shell, *The Job: Work and Its Future in a Time of Radical Change* (Penguin Random House, 2018).
[12] Susan Pinker, *The Village Effect: Why Face-to-Face Contact Matters.* 2nd ed. (Atlantic Books, 2015).

for community organizing, advocacy, and movement-building.[13] There really is power in numbers, especially for young people who lack the social capital needed to access certain economic opportunities, but who still choose to fight for a more fair and just world.

In the book, *The 100-Year Life*, authors Lynda Gratton and Andrew Scott encourage readers to rethink the importance of strong, lasting friendships and familial ties. With so much changing, the constancy and potency of lifelines will support today's kids across many seasons and situations. The people caring for young people today—mentoring, befriending, and being there for them—may also be the ones down the road encouraging them to go back to school, or to keep applying for jobs when it seems none are available. Lifelines will help young people to pause, rest, reset, and recreate whenever life demands it.

WHERE TO FIND LIFELINES

- At home and in the neighborhood. Many lifelines are family and community members.
- Mentorship programs, "buddy" programs, and other peer support groups.
- Extracurriculars and enrichment activities. These include school clubs and sports.
- Out-of-school time programs. These include after school programs and summer camps.
- At school, in class, and during larger group times, including lunch and recess.
- During group activities and assignments.

Door Openers

Jon Zaff and Forrest Moore have been working together for a long time. Jon is a professor at Boston University, in the Wheelock College of Education & Human Development; Forrest works for Chapin Hall, at the University of Chicago. For years, both held senior roles at America's Promise Alliance, a leading organization started by General Colin Powell and his wife Alma,

---

[13]Daniel Hunter, *Building a Movement to End the New Jim Crow: An Organizing Guide* (Hyrax Publishing, 2015).

which made a name for itself by running a national campaign to improve US high school graduation rates.

While at America's Promise, Jon and Forrest, along with their research team at the Center for Promise, spent time on the road meeting young people and hearing their experiences of staying in school or dropping out. From those encounters, the team produced two national studies and two national surveys.[14] They surveyed roughly 3,000 young people and spoke to hundreds more. The team was struck by how almost all talked as much about the people in their lives as their situations. For those who went on to graduate, many credited parents, caring teachers, close friends, or coaches. And those who didn't, talked about the social supports they needed, but never got.

As Jon and Forrest looked deeper, they found that youth who did well in school had strong lifelines along with something more. Story after story showed how lifelines kept young people going, but a web of other social connections was crucial for finding new and better opportunities. For many, this "anchor & web" support network—a concept later developed by Jon and his colleague Shannon Varga, while working together at the CERES Institute for Children & Youth[15]—was a combination of people and programs. Anchoring lifelines might include any number of family members, teachers, friends or coaches, while a web of door openers was found through an afterschool club or college access program. Through their work, Jon and Forrest came to understand that lifelines offered young people critical social bonds while "door openers" offered social bridges that would otherwise be hard or impossible to find and access.[16]

Finding Door Openers

Young people from well-resourced families and communities often have more door openers than they need. Their parents, parents' friends, relatives,

---

[14] The reports on the research and results were "Don't Call Them Dropouts" and "Don't Quit on Me." Both were produced by America's Promise Alliance.

[15] Shannon M. Varga and Jonathan F. Zaff, "Webs of Support: An Integrative Framework of Relationships, Social Networks, and Social Support for Positive Youth Development," *Adolescent Research Review* 3 (2018): 1–11. https://doi.org/10.1007/s40894-017-0076-x.

[16] Sam M. Intrator and Don Siegel, *The Quest for Mastery: Positive Youth Development Through Out-of-School Programs* (Boston: Harvard Education Press, 2014).

classmates, classmates' families and schools offer ample connections and social capital-building opportunities.

The most profound example I ever witnessed was during a work trip to Houston. I was staying at the historic Houstonian hotel, famous for once housing President George H.W. Bush and wife, Barbara. Hotel guests get free access to an exclusive athletic club on the hotel property. While we were there, one curious colleague learned that the annual club membership ranges from $20,000 to $30,000 per year.

I swim, so I was thrilled to learn that I could use the club's lap pool. As soon as my meetings ended, I dashed over to the club. It was around 3 P.M. and the facility was buzzing with after school activities. Kids were meeting with tutors in the cafe, taking private tennis and swimming lessons, and playing basketball on the high-polished courts. After my swim, I grabbed a bite to eat, and eavesdropped a bit on a tutoring session. It must have been for the ACT or SAT, because the tutor was focused not on content knowledge, but on tricks for raising his client's score. Throughout the session, at least a dozen young people walked by and waved to the tutor, striking me as likely clients of his.

That cafe experience reminded me how opportunities abound for the social elite. I have no doubt that business deals and summer internships are found on the Houstonian's basketball courts, and that practice interviews for elite colleges happen in the cafe, while still wearing gym clothes. These athletic clubs are in every city across America, a sign of status and station for those who belong. Within these rooms and on these courts, "door opening" opportunities happen that will never be publicly posted or known outside of insiders' social circles.

This typifies what Llana Gershon found while researching *Down and Out in the New Economy;* when it comes to getting the best education and employment opportunities, reputation and relationships are more important than skills and qualifications.[17] Young people born into privilege unknowingly hoard opportunities because of availability,

---

[17] Llana Gershon, *Down and Out in the New Economy: How People Find (or Don't Find) Work Today* (The University of Chicago Press, 2017).

awareness, and preferential access. Then access is subsequently denied to nonmembers, who couldn't get in first or at all, because they were not from the right family, community, or social group.

Young people from families that struggle to get by and who have parents that work long hours at low-wage jobs often have no clue about the types of "at the club" door-opening opportunities that pass them by—sometimes just minutes from their homes and neighborhoods. Back at the Houstonian, I wasn't surprised when a young woman from our meeting—local to the area, showed up to the hotel shocked that it was so close to her home. She had never even heard of it.

We can architect these "at the club" connections through quality social capital and relationship-building programs. These can happen via coach and tutor relationships, mentoring and internship programs, and sports participation, all of which build social networks, status, and even future scholarship opportunities. These programs end up being equity extenders, enabling kids whose parents can't afford a club membership to benefit from social bridging that leads to new opportunities and upward mobility.

My friend and colleague, Julia Freeland Fisher, has taught me that these deliberately designed social connections offer the supports, information, and endorsements necessary for opening doors to new interests, opportunities, and careers.[18]

In her research, Julia has found that there are also emerging digital tools to facilitate or otherwise support door opener introductions. These are especially important given how frequent digital experiences will be moving forward. Some of these, including Nepris and Educurious, put young people in touch with experts from their fields of interest. Others offer virtual work-based learning experiences, which can offer important on-ramps to future careers and professional networks. These digital tools are hugely promising, not as much for their technological prowess as for

---

[18] Freeland Fisher and Fisher, *Who You Know: Unlocking Innovations That Expand Students' Networks.*

the potential that they can break through historic cost and geographic barriers to offer door openers where they were previously out of reach.

WHERE TO FIND DOOR OPENERS

- Before- and after-school clubs and athletics
- Mentorship and internship programs
- In-person or online career pathways opportunities, including job shadowing and work-based learning programs
- School-community partnership programs, especially with local employers and colleges
- Dual enrollment programs and early college opportunities

Navigators

Sometimes I use Facebook to find the information I need. There are several local "Moms groups"—each with hundreds or thousands of members with a story to share, opinion to offer, or tip to trade. They provide me with proximity and affinity benefits. These are other women in my town, raising kids, who have similar questions and concerns.

Here are some popular questions that routinely pop up:

- "Help, I need a new pediatrician. My current one isn't a good fit. Who do you recommend?"
- "Does anyone know if the flu is going around? My son has been sick for the past week, and even though I got him vaccinated, I think I should get him tested."
- "Recommendations on where my spouse and I should go out for dinner? We haven't been on a date in forever."[19]

These Facebook groups are one way social media works for me. These women are in a similar life stage, and their kids are in my kids' schools,

---

[19] Obviously, these questions have changed pretty dramatically since COVID-19 started. At the time of this writing, these groups are mostly full of questions and concerns related to the reopening of schools and where to find toilet paper.

camps, and germ radius. The similarity of our situations lends a certain level of trust and openness.

This kind of online, networked navigational tool requires a level of access, discretion, and critical thinking. I'm not going to take everyone's advice and I'm not going to overly share information about my children. I am, however, going to keep these groups as a part of my social repository, a place where I can get the localized recommendations I need.

This is not where I would go for professional advice. Few people in my community work for national organizations and no one close by does my type of work. If I need professional guidance, I look to my more geographically distributed network of connections—colleagues, acquaintances, and former co-workers—who primarily live in America's big cities.

As a whole, these people make up my navigational network. Some of my navigators are lifelines. This includes some longtime mentors who advise me professionally and personally. There are also colleagues who are friends and fellow parents; they can provide valuable insights and comfort on both work and kid dilemmas. Then there are one-and-done navigators; these are people I seek out for very specific reasons. This could be for health, legal, or financial issues, or requests for information on a professional need or opportunity.

In tomorrow's rapidly changing world, I predict the most important navigators will be peers or near peers. While there will continue to be immense value in multigenerational lifelines, people will need navigational support from those who are also navigating similar situations, in real time, but maybe just a step or two ahead. Additionally, it will become increasingly important to locate and connect with navigators virtually and at a distance.

Human Navigators and the Art of Way finding

There is nothing more powerful than meeting someone who really gets you. It ignites an immediate energy born of authentic connection—a social and emotional buzz. Throughout life, we need people who understand us because they know where we are coming from. They are able to direct us in ways that feel familiar. These navigators are those who have trudged similar roads to our own.

As the world spins and shifts, these types of navigators will become harder to come by. This is because so many of the roads will be new. In the future, we may see navigators' roles evolve. Instead of providing a blue-print for how to make it through something, tomorrow's navigators may need to focus more on the art of wayfinding.

As a native Hawaiian, I have always been curious about how a group of Polynesian journeyers left Tahiti and found dots in the middle of the ocean, islands including Hawaii, without a compass, map, or GPS. Instead, they were taught how to wayfind—exploration that requires observation, intuition, the stars, and other signs in nature to tell them where to go.

In tomorrow's world, today's kids will be navigating together, way-finding in search of a long and livable life.

The Rise of Digital Navigators

Today's kids are growing up in the age of digital assistants. Alexa and Siri can direct them from one place to the next, answer questions, tell funny jokes, and provide guidance on whether or not certain health symptoms warrant a trip to the doctor. Beyond these popular household digital assistants, there are many other digital navigational assistants coming on the market. Apps that track our vitals and make recommendations for how to modify diet and when to exercise. Behavioral nudging programs that prompt us to do certain things—like remembering to apply to college, and then for financial aid; or checking in with our bodies and breath, through preprogrammed meditations and mindfulness exercises.

Digital navigators are going to become increasingly common. There are some really thoughtful hybrid models that blend no-to-low-cost, powerful technology and still-essential human interactions. One of my favorites is my colleague Jaime-Alexis Fowler's organization, Empower Work.

Before she launched, Jaime-Alexis and her team interviewed hun-dreds of people across the country about who they turn to when facing a tough or embarrassing work situation. They wanted to know: What do people need at these critical moments? They found that people with lower amounts of social capital (fewer lifelines, door openers and navigators) had very few, if any, places to go to for help.

Believing every person deserves free, high-quality support and advice during challenging and confusing times, they created a digital platform that operates by using text messages or web chat. If people need work advice (e.g., "I think my boss is treating me unfairly, what do I do?"; "Something happened at work today, can you tell me if it's harassment?"), they text or send an online message to one of Empower Work's trained volunteers. From there, the volunteers follow a protocol of various prompts and questions to provide real-time virtual guidance on how to handle the situation and what to do next. In this case, technology and a digital platform power human-to-human navigational interaction.

Meanwhile, technical navigation (e.g., how do I apply for this program? Where do I go to find a job?) is increasingly handled by behind-the-scenes artificial intelligence technology, mostly chatbots. As AI continues to get more sophisticated, machine navigators for young people will be used in ways currently reserved for people. The same technology that assists a doctor in running a set of complicated symptoms against empirical studies to generate possible diagnoses, may one day be able to run every available scholarship opportunity for a young person, based on personal background and interests.

WHERE TO FIND NAVIGATORS

- At home and in the neighborhood
- Extracurriculars, including clubs, sports, and other activities
- Online platforms that provide real-time guiding, coaching, and nudging
- Counseling and advising services, both humans and bots
- Mentorship and internship programs

Connections as Currency

In the book *Behave,* Robert Sapolsky—a neurobiologist and primatologist—describes young people as biologically wired with the "frantic need to belong." While networks act as the connective tissue for all of us, they are, by design, especially important for young people.[20] Survival and status depend on who young people know and who those people know. Identity and purpose are defined by who we affiliate with. Social network

---

[20] Julia Hobsbawm, *Fully Connected: Social Health in an Age of Overload* (Bloomsbury, 2018).

affiliations can be structured—including neighborhoods, groups, political parties, and fraternal organizations; and unstructured, including who our friends are, what musicians we are fans of, or our alumni status.

Our social networks are where we seek out advice, introductions, new economic opportunities, and even more connections. Our networks tell us what is normal and acceptable, what we should expect, and what is within our reach. Generally speaking, the more connected someone is, the more opportunities they have. The higher status the network, the more lucrative—and often, substantial—the opportunities.

Our networks of lifelines, door openers, and navigators are worth something. This value is known as social capital, or social worth. Plenty of research shows that friends, family, and associates are the way we find our next, best opportunity. Network forces are economic mobilizers. Social capital brings advantages, and a lack of it perpetuates inequity.

There are those born into families with high-value social networks. These young people are socially wealthy from the start. It is like having a social trust fund established at birth. Prestigious social connections make it easier to get into high-demand programs, elite colleges, competitive internships, and jobs. Because of historic racism and exclusionary practice, those who have the most social wealth tend to be white and financially well-off.

Consider Ivy League "legacy admissions"—this is when a high school graduate's chance of getting into a university, like Harvard or Yale, more than doubles because family members are alumni and donors. If they get in and graduate, that Ivy League degree pulls in even more social and economic dividends (just like real interest and dividends, this is a cycle of ever-increasing prestige and pedigree). It's like a real-life version of the game Chutes and Ladders. In life, those with the most social capital experience accelerated economic mobility—steering clear of chutes and reaching every ladder.

At the other end of the spectrum are those born into families with very little social capital. The people they are surrounded by struggle to find and keep work. Everyone is in need of better opportunities. For these kids, the chutes abound. Getting into competitive programs, elite colleges, and competitive internships and jobs feels like a pipe dream, rather than presumption.

Social networks accrue interest—if you're born with shares of a valuable stock, you acquire the benefits without ever having to make the expense. In America's social class system, some have plenty of social network stock options, connecting with inside traders who know the rules, and many more have never made it to our social Wall Street.[21]

Who You Know

In their book, *Who You Know: Unlocking Innovations that Expand Students' Networks,* Julia Freeland Fisher and her husband and co-writer, Daniel Fisher, argue that learning environments need to be deliberately designed in ways that enable young people to build social networks that increase their social capital. Tomorrow will be a more volatile and riskier world. Making it and moving ahead will have to do with skill and personality, as well as being able to tap into a network of people who can offer immediate options and opportunities for advancement.

The places young people learn are also where they build relationships and broker new connections. As Julia and Daniel point out, new advances in digital and online tools and platforms expand that learning ecosystem even more, enabling a social space where young people can connect with each other, in person and online.

Our virtual and in-person learning settings need to be recognized as the social marketplaces they are. Once acknowledged, we can plan for ways young people can connect with people from different networks and neighborhoods, forging and nurturing long-term relationships that provide social support and necessary bridges to future opportunities. A few spaces ripe for social capital building are mentorship and internship programs, career pathways programs, arts and athletics, and other school–community partnership offerings.[22]

Doing this work requires us to understand the role of social class, culture, and cues. To make it, young people will need to be able to travel and translate across a number of social settings and situations. We can support those who need more social capital by teaching them ways to operate in new and different social settings.

---

[21] To learn more about the connection between a young person's social networks and racial and economic background, I recommend checking out research done by Raj Chetty, Robert Putnam, and Richard Reeves.

[22] Freeland Fisher and Fisher, *Who You Know: Unlocking Innovations That Expand Students' Networks.*

As Harvard Graduate School of Education professor, Anthony Abraham Jack, described in a powerful *New York Times Magazine* commentary, being a low-income student at Amherst College was tough in a number of ways. In addition to the inadequate financial supports Jack received, he confronted ongoing cultural and social barriers. For example, he recalls not knowing what it meant to "get coffee" with a professor—who pays, why do you do it, and how does it work?[23]

There are similar stories shared by many who venture and bridge into social classes and cultures different from the ones they grew up in. Building young people's social lexicon and cultural toolbox is another part of building their social capital. To be agents of their own futures, young people will need social networks and relationships that sustain, connections that catalyze, and tools that enable translation across settings, classes, and cultures.

In the end, *connections* may end up being the most valuable currency young people can have and use in adulthood. They are powerful on their own and they ratchet up the value of credentials, competencies, and cash. Today's kids might need a college credential to qualify for a job, but a great group of friends will make the experience rich and worthwhile, and a degree from a well-respected and recognized institution could put their resume on the top of the stack. Cash can be used to buy things, but when it is used to purchase a membership, it can elevate status and expand perceived worth and access to future opportunities. Being competent is crucial for getting the job done, but having a great reputation is how to get promoted.

Social capital is an often understated but overly important part of the opportunity transactions young people need to make it in life.

---

[23] Anthony Abraham Jack, "I Was a Low-Income College Student. Classes Weren't the Hard Part," *The New York Times*, September 10, 2019. https://www.nytimes.com/interactive/2019/09/10/magazine/college-inequality.html.

CHAPTER 5

Credentials

credential: *the diploma, degrees and certificates someone has*

Growing up, I believed there were two credentialing pathways into adulthood: either you graduate high school and go to college right away; or, you graduate high school, work for a few years, and eventually enroll in night classes at the local community college. I was somewhat aware of other credentialing opportunities but didn't consider them "college;" this included things like occupational licenses, training for a certain job in the military, apprenticeships, or getting a job-specific certificate or endorsement.

For years, education's North Star has been high schoolers graduating and going to a four-year accredited university. Many of us have long operated under the assumption that the better the school—and more recognized the name—the better the future.

In wealthy communities, going to college after high school is the de facto choice. Young people who go straight to work or enlist are seen as anomalies—often leaving friends and family to wonder what went wrong— did they have maturity issues? Problems at home? Were they not cut out for the college environment?

For America's wealthiest, not going to college is a choice.

For young people who grow up poor, college is the goal but not always a choice.

When I ran a school in St. Louis, students regularly told me about the people they knew who had been top-performers at local high schools, only to go to college far away and return—ashamed and in debt—mid-semester. There were many reasons why that happened, some financial, some cultural, all understandable. Too often, these young people went to college lacking the resources, supports, and preparation they needed to stick with it and make it to graduation.

My husband and I experienced this with our nephew. He is supremely talented in the arts. He graduated from a city magnet school as class president, with honors. After high school graduation, he packed his things and headed to art school in Chicago. Then the more hidden costs of college assailed him, including unexpected expenses like dinners with friends; buying clothes, costumes, and supplies; and paying for housing. He was home a year later.

Educators are now pulling back from the popular stance that every student should strive for a four-year college degree. Many now see the personal toll of sending an unprepared student away, like my nephew, to follow a North Star without the resources needed for the journey. On the other side, there are also those who make it through college, finish and graduate, but then can't find a good job, leaving them to question whether it was really worth it.

Is a College Degree Still Worth It?

If we are going to reconsider the North Star, we have to consider the vast changes happening in the US credentialing marketplace against the evidence on whether a college degree is a worthwhile investment.

As of today, earning a traditional postsecondary degree—an associate or bachelor's degree from an accredited school—still improves your chances for getting a good job and it can also improve economic security, family stability, and financial independence.

As of 2020, more than half of all jobs required a college degree,[1] and most new jobs went to people who already had a postsecondary credential. Although a credential may lead to debt in the short-term, it often pays off over time.[2] In 2019, the "college wage premium" showed that workers with

---

[1] Credential Engine, "Counting US Postsecondary and Secondary Credentials," Credential Engine, September 2019. https://credentialengine.org/wp-content/uploads/2019/09/Counting-US-Postsecondary-and-Secondary-Credentials_190925_FINAL.pdf.
[2] The Georgetown University *Center on Education and the Workforce* is a great resource for learning more about the economic and social benefits of postsecondary credentials.

a bachelor's degree made roughly $78,000 per year, while those without a postsecondary credential made $45,000.[3] In the long term, a traditional college degree may not be necessary, but some type of postsecondary credential seems to be.

It is left to be seen whether these benefits will change. While most jobs go to credential earners, there are new jobs available every day that don't require a degree. Many of them, however, appear to be gig work or low-wage jobs. On the other hand, some employers—including my own—are removing degree requirements from job postings, replacing them with the competencies that reflect the position.

Young people may be able to make it without a credential, but it is a real risk that will require an overabundance of the other currencies—competencies, connections, and cash—in its place. Instead of forgoing this currency because of cost concerns or other barriers, young people should learn how many different options are available, then set realistic expectations and find something that works for them.

Diplomas

Before entering the postsecondary credentialing marketplace, a young person must earn a high school diploma or General Equivalency Diploma (GED). Many young people see this first credential as their golden ticket to a good life. And yet, it is not always a reliable measure of readiness for life after high school. Diplomas are usually *completion credentials*, representing a combination of completed coursework, time spent in class, and mastering academic standards. This doesn't always translate into the full set of knowledge, skills, and experiences they need to be prepared for college or work. In credential speak, we would say the high school diploma has inconsistent *market value*.

---

[3] Bento J. Lobo and Lisa A. Burke-Smalley, "An Empirical Investigation of the Financial Value of a College Degree," *Education Economics* 26 (1)(2018): 78–92. https://doi.org/10.10 80/09645292.2017.1332167.

Pushed and Pulled Out

In 2007, I was starting a school for young people who had disconnected from other public high schools.[4] As we enrolled our first class, we noticed big gaps between our students' grade assignment—per their transcripts— and how they performed academically. Our students came from more than 15 area high schools, and they were all officially in 10th–12th grade. As we got to know them, we found that most performed many grade levels behind what their transcripts told us. Far too many lacked even basic knowledge and skills.

A confusing combination of low grades (Cs, Ds), incompletes, and partial credits had kept them on the path to graduation even though they weren't academically ready. We were shocked. We had started our school because we knew students were being pushed or pulled *out* of school because of life. We weren't expecting how many of them had also been pushed or pulled *through* school because of policy.[5]

The Opportunity Myth

In 2018, the national education nonprofit TNTP, released: *The Opportunity Myth: What Students Can Show Us about How School Is Letting Them Down—and How to Fix It.* This report focused on what happened to students who stayed in high school and earned their high school diplomas. The report showed that almost half of all graduates got a diploma but still had to take remedial college courses. For many, these non-credit-bearing courses were a fast way to dry up financial aid without advancing toward a degree. Students who ended up in remedial classes were far more likely to drop out of college.

---

[4] Today, these young people are often referred to as *opportunity youth*. The number of young people disconnected from school and work had been dropping before COVID-19, but the numbers more than doubled, during the first six months of the pandemic. It was a dramatic reminder of how many young people are vulnerable to life situations that can push or pull them away from the learning and work opportunities they need.

[5] This could get much worse in future years. Because of COVID-19-related school closures, many school districts passed policies to graduate students or pass them to the next grade, so long as they completed the minimum requirements. While this may support student engagement and morale in the short-term, in the long-term it could lead to young people entering adulthood without critical knowledge and skills, even if they have passing grades and a high school diploma.

TNTP said the "Opportunity Myth" is that millions of students stay in school, do what is asked of them, graduate, and still go on to struggle.

The high school teachers and administrators I have spoken to, agree with this myth. These educators know that some of the academic standards they teach are more relevant in real life than others, and that grades are not always accurate measures of learning. Teachers confessed to doing whatever their departments, districts, or states require of them— even when they believed those requirements were outdated or flawed. A number told me they have considered leaving the profession because they don't always feel they have the freedom to prepare students in the ways they know are needed.

Making Diplomas Count

There is hope. Pioneering schools and districts across the US are busting the Opportunity Myth and revamping their graduation requirements, committed to awarding graduates a more modern high school diploma, which reflects the prerequisites for life after high school.

A number of those places are in Virginia.

Back in 2014, earning a Virginia high school diploma meant that students had completed required coursework, checked off a long list of content standards and taken 32 standardized tests. Virginia's focus on high academic standards and testing had led—unintentionally—to a culture of completion and compliance over one of student competence and preparedness.

Then Governor Terry McAuliffe appointed Steve Staples as state superintendent. Staples wanted to see the Virginia high school diploma as a credential valued by employers, colleges, and universities. During his tenure, Staples worked within every level of education to evolve Virginia's graduation requirements. In the end, the state adopted a *Profile of a Virginia Graduate*. This profile revisited required content knowledge and standards, confirming relevancy, and then expanded requirements to include essential experiences and skills needed for a rapidly changing world.

The freshman class of 2018 kicked off high school with these new state graduation requirements in place. Their high school experience now includes coursework, work-based learning, service-learning, and the development of five competencies that Virginia employers and higher education leaders felt were crucial for future success: critical thinking, collaboration, citizenship, creative thinking, and communication.

With state requirements in place, Virginia school districts initiated their own efforts, customizing graduation requirements to fit their community context and student needs:

- In Salem—a small city in Virginia's Blue Ridge—Superintendent Alan Seibert and his team decided that students needed to graduate with a "diploma and a plan"; they leveraged state changes as an opportunity to deliver a more personalized education to students, focusing on competency attainment and robust career pathways.
- In Cumberland—a working class, rural community outside of Richmond—Superintendent Amy Griffin, worked with community leaders to build a local *Profile of a Cumberland Graduate*, which included a "passion project" for juniors and seniors to connect classwork, the five Cs, and community service.
- In Hampton—a city near Norfolk—the school district, under the leadership of Superintendent Jeff Smith, rolled out 16 career academies connected to more than 40 local, high-demand occupational pathways; the state profile was used as the guiding framework for designing a high school experience that balanced content delivery and career development.

Salem's superintendent once explained the importance of modernizing the diploma to me this way: "*In the 1990s, when [Virginia's standardized] assessments were built, arthroscopic surgery was not widely used. Today it is, and we know it works and is often the very best thing for patients. If surgeons and diagnosticians are using new tools, then why are we still using vestiges from the 1990s?*"

Five Ways to Modernize the High School Diploma

- Petition your school district's administration and board to cut back on unnecessary standardized testing requirements and encourage them to update graduation requirements to better reflect postsecondary education and labor market demands.
- Advocate for (or help to develop) a district policy that requires the district to regularly review and revise graduation requirements. As postsecondary education and work changes so should graduation requirements.
- Invite postsecondary education leaders and employers to discussions on what graduates need; invite them to contribute to revisions on graduation requirements. They know better than most what is needed after high school.
- If you are not already, consider a competency- or performance-based diploma. First step: make sure your district has eliminated harmful seat-time requirements; second step: amend course and credit requirements to focus on proficiency and enable students to move on when ready.
- Make sure graduation requirements include preparatory experiences that familiarize young people with the postsecondary world. This could include work-based learning, career pathways, and service learning.

The US Credentialing Marketplace

In 2016, I was directing a national campaign—Connecting Credentials—which brought together postsecondary credentialing actors across the US, in an attempt to make the credentialing marketplace more organized, equitable, and inclusive. The campaign started as a response to dramatic changes in the higher education world. The number of credentialing opportunities had skyrocketed, and the credentialing "marketplace" was increasingly chaotic and hard to navigate. Instead of a straightforward path into and through college, you could suddenly consider new options with techie names, like micro- and nano-degrees, badges, bootcamps, and MOOCs.

Two years in, one of our campaign co-sponsors, Credentialing Engine, put out a report suggesting there were more than 300,000 different credentials in the United States. Just one year later, that number had doubled, with 2019 counts coming in around 750,000.[6] It is a gargantuan task to keep track and make sense of this growing marketplace of postsecondary options, let alone to sift through and figure out which credentials are best.

In tomorrow's world, these credentialing numbers will continue to go up, and the types of credentialing opportunities will be in constant flux. Economic volatility will mean that there are always adults seeking out new or better work and needing to upgrade or validate their knowledge and skills in order to compete. This demand will bring more credentialing vendors and different credentials into the market, making it even more vast and complex.

Increasingly, going to college or pursuing a postsecondary credential will feel like shopping on a poorly organized Amazon, complete with having to search for what you want, decide whether it's a good deal, compare prices, read reviews, and know which models and features are worth the expense.

Becoming Credential Consumers

Today's kids must understand that they are consumers in the US credentialing marketplace. It will be about credential readiness, which goes beyond college readiness. They are purchasing postsecondary products, which will require smart consumer behaviors. Young people need to be able to tell a good credentialing provider from a bad one; they need tools to help them figure out whether the cost of a credential is worth it. In this market, for-profit vendors and organizations will offer almost as many options as colleges and universities. One day, those "nontraditional" providers could dominate the market.

---

[6] Credential Engine, *Counting US Postsecondary and Secondary Credentials*.

This is what the US credentialing marketplace was offering as of 2019:

US Credentialing Marketplace—Credentials by Type[7]

	Colleges & Universities	MOOC Providers	Non-Academic Organizations	High Schools
Number of Credentials Offered	370,020	7,132	315,067	46,209
Types of Credentials	· Degrees and Certificates	· Micro-credentials · Degrees from foreign universities · Course completion certificates (e.g., EdX or Coursera)	· Occupational licenses · Industry-recognized certifications · Military certifications · Registered and unregistered apprenticeships · Coding bootcamp completion certificates · Online course completion certificates · Digital badges	· Diplomas

Imagine you want to buy a book. You go to Amazon, where there are millions of titles to choose from. Amazon automatically populates your screen with what your search and purchase history says you like. From there, it only takes a couple clicks and a few minutes to find what you want. You limit results by reading style (hardback, paper copy, Kindle), genre, author, price, and maybe best reviewed. You even set up an email notification to alert you to new releases from your favorite authors.

The US credentialing marketplace is not yet powered by this type of artificial intelligence or order and organization. Young people will not find it easy to locate and choose the best credentials. They need to rely on their human intelligence to make good decisions from among hundreds of thousands of available options.

---

7 Ibid.

Five Questions to Ask When Choosing a Credential

Here are the *five consumer questions* young people should ask before deciding on a credential:

1. Do I really need this?
2. What does this come with?
3. How long will this last?
4. How does this compare to others like it?
5. Can I afford this?

Do I Really Need This Credential?

Young people need to become discriminating credential consumers. The credential they choose has to make sense, given the time and resources they have, their situations, preferences, interests, and goals. Some credentials take a few weeks and others many years. Some providers allow you to start and stop as needed, while others expect you to do everything in one go. Credentials cover hundreds of different topics and industries. They can be earned on campuses, in office buildings, community settings, or at home. Credentials can be completed in person, online—or both. When COVID-19 forced colleges into emergency remote learning, everything moved online—and a number of programs will stay that way.

Young people need to know their shopping preferences and stipulations before entering the marketplace. As my friend and colleague Amber Garrison Duncan, a strategy director at Lumina Foundation, explains: Shopping the credentialing marketplace is about enabling young people to take the first or next step they need, rather than a once-in-a-lifetime career choice.

Credentials are not an end within themselves, they are an enabler of future opportunities.

Static, Springboard, and Lifetime Opportunities

At JFF, my colleague Sara Lamback partnered with Burning Glass Technologies to demonstrate how American workers get into middle-skill jobs—that is, jobs that require some type of education or training beyond a high school diploma and that pay a living wage or more. She and the Burning Glass team analyzed more than 4 million resumes. They found three distinct types of middle-skill roles: lifetime jobs, which are their own careers (e.g., dental hygienists); springboard jobs, which lead to careers (e.g., becoming a bookkeeper and moving on to become an accountant); and static jobs, which don't lead to careers, and are less stable and lower paying (e.g., a machine operator).

Taking Amber's notion that credentials should be viewed as a first or next step, we can apply this framework to evaluate various credentials against the future economic benefits they might provide. When deciding whether a credential is worth it, young people might ask themselves whether the credential will lead to the static, springboard, or lifetime job opportunities they need:

- **Will this credential lead to the *static job opportunities* I need?** These might be entry-level completion credentials that qualify a young person for a job that only serves to pay the bills. This could be a certificate of completion to drive for a gig company or a training certificate to be a medical assistant. These credentials don't lead to career-building opportunities but can lead to helpful forms of employment and earnings while pursuing another economic opportunity.
- **Will this credential lead to the *springboard job opportunities* I need?** These credentials position someone for entry-level jobs in the career area they want to work in long-term. A common springboard credential is the CompTIA A+ certification, usually offered at a local community college. Workers with an A+ certification are prepared for entry-level positions in IT and positioned to earn more advanced credentials later on. Springboard credentialing opportunities should be highly "stackable." This is a credentialing term that means a credential connects to another one, stacking—like blocks—to better work and wages.
- **Is this credential going to lead to the *lifetime job opportunity* I need?** These credentials put young people on a career path—one that provides some degree of job stability and solid earnings. These credentials have historically been found on college campuses,

but increasingly, non-academic providers offer them, too. They also include a number of registered apprenticeships. Examples might include credentials to become a dental hygienist, welder, or machinist.

When considering credentialing options, beware the *"dead-end" credential!* These are credentials that lead to jobs that do not pay a living wage and will likely disappear because of disruption, automation, or other environmental and economic forces. As with anything, it is possible for young people to have their hearts set on a particular degree path or future job. If that happens to be associated with a dead-end credential, talk through what this means and examine the risks. Another "dead-end" concern would be specifically for young people who are undocumented. If their status will get in the way of being able to take national boards or other certifying requirements, then certain credentials may not be worth consideration.

One way to decide which credentials to pursue is to look at local labor market data. You can do this by going to the US Department of Labor's O-NET database. Look for *high-growth* and *high-demand* industries and occupations wherever a young person plans to live, and then review the average earnings in those related positions. This will definitely help avoid those dead-end credentials. High-growth and high-demand jobs change with the local environment and economy, so be sure your search findings are up to date.

After a disaster, whether a natural disaster or something like COVID-19, local economies can undergo rapid and dramatic changes. In these cases, it can be hard to keep labor market data up to date. If this happens, reach out to local employers and workforce development agencies and ask for their help.

What Does This Credential Come With?

A credential is more valuable when it connects to the other currencies—competencies, connections, and cash. As a consumer, young people should find out what competencies they will develop or strengthen while pursuing the credential. Will those competencies make them more competitive in the job market? Assist them on the job? Will they transfer to other fields if and when the young person needs to find something new?

One way to help young people figure this out is to look at a course catalog or other materials that break down class offerings and what students can expect to learn and do. Some credentials, especially occupational licenses and apprenticeships, come with extensive on-the-job experience and training, along with mentorship and a culminating certification.

Credentials can also bring strong connections by way of brand power and alumni networks. From a consumer perspective, this is a life-altering version of the difference between an Oreo cookie and a chocolate-and-creme cookie substitute. Even though it's often unintentional, employers often show a preferential bias for people who graduated from well-known and elite schools (e.g., Harvard University); there is an underlying assumption that those workers will be better and smarter employees.

Credentials from top colleges carry the social power and sway of institutional affiliation. Increasingly, this is true of non-academic credentialing providers. For instance, Google offers an IT Support Professional Certificate through the for-profit online learning platform, Coursera. A network of colleges and nonprofits provide postsecondary learners with free access to this certificate. Completers get a credential from Google, not the partnering nonprofit or college. Even though Google is a marketing company and not an IT support company, the Google brand brings its own level of credibility and labor market value, perhaps even more powerful than the quality of the credentialing content or learning experience.

Lastly, young people should consider what cash supports and resources a credential comes with, comparing that with what they need. Is financial assistance available? How about counseling? Advising or job placement services? Are there practical resources or connections to help with childcare, food, or housing? These are items that can initially seem peripheral but end up being central to whether or not the young person succeeds.

How Long Will This Credential Last?

In a world with ever-changing demands and economic conditions, today's kids must consider how long their credential will be valuable in the labor market. Do they think this is something that will put them on a path to future work opportunities or continuing education? Or, is it possible that the credentialing opportunity will lead them in the opposite direction, toward jobs that are time stamped, or about to disappear?

Consider my consumer adventures in purchasing lasting luggage, as someone who is on the road a lot for work. I started with the least expensive and easiest-to-find option. It quickly wore out. My next option was a slight step up but lacked the compartments I needed to hold my stuff. Within a couple years, I had spent more on poorly made luggage that didn't fit my lifestyle, than if I had just invested in one "lifetime" item from the start. Choosing the right credential has some striking similarities to choosing the right luggage:

- If it's affordable and the purchase will pay for itself over time, it can be worth spending more money up front.
- Get what is really needed. Look for the add-ons and features that match lifestyle, demands, and future ambitions.
- Look for enduring quality and durability.
- Purchases should match what is needed now and ideally what is desired for the future.

My colleague's framework of static, springboard, or lifetime job opportunities makes it clear that young people do not need to invest in a lifetime credential if that doesn't match their foreseeable future or present needs. They should, however, think about whether their credential is something they can build on over time—stackability, like a luggage set—can be purchased in installments.

Young people might also start a credential and realize it isn't for them. In credentialing terms, these situations benefit from strong *transfer and articulation* agreements. This means being able to transfer institutions but still get credit for whatever was already accomplished. It can be helpful to think through this possibility on the front-end.

How Does This Credential Compare with Others Like It?

Beyond future job prospects, young people should also enjoy their credentialing experience. This is a serious investment, and one that should bring personal satisfaction for years to come. This means finding an opportunity that offers high-quality learning opportunities—whether that is happening in-person or online—along with a culture and environment that matches the young person's wants and needs.

Let's say a young person wants to get a general degree somewhere close to home. They apply to four local universities and amazingly, get accepted into all four institutions. They need to evaluate and compare the learning experience and environment before making a final decision:

Quality of Learning

When young people have the luxury of choice, they should first consider what type of learning experience they want and need. Then, they should research class and course offerings, structure, and instructors. Basic internet research and conversations with admissions counselors or current students and alumni are all good ways to do this. Young people who are parents, or those with disabilities or health concerns, should find out what learning supports and accommodations are available, if they are good, and how easy they are to access. This is particularly important for newer credentialing providers. Often, these providers are not accredited or publicly mandated to offer learning supports and services. Finally, it is worth reviewing credential completion data, and—if it is available—employment information on alumni. Getting a postsecondary credential should be personally meaningful and economically valuable.

Type of Environment

Relationships, vibe, and culture can be as important as the quality of the learning experience. Young people are more likely to enjoy and complete their credential if they feel welcome and know they belong. Cultural responsiveness and community supports matter. Young people can get a sense of what to expect by talking to others who have experienced the credentialing provider or the specific credentialing opportunity. These conversations can reveal what life is like on the ground, and whether it is a good fit for what the young person wants and needs. If there is no one in the young person's personal network to ask, consider reaching out to current staff or students.

Can I Afford This Credential?

The final question young people must ask, is whether the credential is something they can pay for and whether it will pay off in the end. This is both a financial and emotional decision. Every year, students choose credentials that send them or their families into debt—from which some never recover. This debt causes people to respond in life-altering ways, including remortgaging homes, or struggling with depression and anxiety. Young people have to consider upfront costs and weigh them against potential benefits. Here are some of the more staggering costs associated with getting a postsecondary credential in the US, as of 2020:

- The New York Federal Reserve reports that student loan debt has more than quadrupled since 2005.
- Credentials are least affordable for the middle class. They make too much to qualify for government assistance, but not enough to pay a credential "sticker price."[8]
- The Institute of Higher Education Policy (IHEP) has reported that only six state universities are affordable for working- and middle-class families; they also found that financial aid rarely covers non-tuition costs, such as housing, food, technology, or textbooks.
- Newer credentials, such as nano-degrees and micro-credentials, can have less of a payoff because many employers still don't recognize, understand, or value them.[9]

In the past 40 years, tuition prices have gone up by 1,375 percent. In actual dollars, a college student at a private university in 1980 could expect to pay roughly $100,000 less in college costs than a student today. These huge costs often require taking out large loans. Working adults have described these future debt payments as "crushing," especially when

---

[8] AnnaMaria Androitis, Ken Brown, and Shane Shifflett, "Families Go Deep in Debt to Stay in the Middle Class," *Wall Street Journal*, April 1, 2019. https://www.wsj.com/articles/families-go-deep-in-debt-to-stay-in-the-middle-class-11564673734.
[9] Lilah Burke, "Who's Completing Microcredentials?" *Inside Higher Ed,* November 20, 2019. https://www.insidehighered.com/digital-learning/article/2019/11/20/new-report-offers-analysis-microcredential-completers.

considered in the context of economic fallouts—like the 2008 Recession and COVID-19—and other rising costs, including healthcare, housing, transportation, and dependent care.[10] The financial burden of paying for college or paying off college looms large.

Bottom line: credentials can be expensive—sometimes *really* expensive— and getting one can lead to better work and wages, but also financial distress. Earning a credential is often a high-value achievement and well worth the expense, but only when the upfront financial investment pays off with more personal satisfaction, professional achievement, and financial reward.

I talked this over with a mentor of mine, Greg Darnieder. Greg has been a national leader on college access and affordability issues for years; first in Chicago and later—during the Obama Administration—as a senior advisor to then Secretary of Education Arne Duncan. Greg led the charge to simplify FAFSA and now helps state and district teams improve their college and career readiness strategies.

From Greg's perspective, FAFSA and other forms of financial aid are only one part of the larger financial planning and borrowing strategy required to alleviate financial burdens associated with a postsecondary education. The FAFSA should be situated within a fully comprehensive financial plan that families can use to account and adjust for short- and long-term expenses and debt.

In Greg's experience, this kind of planning is important for all families because credential affordability issues do not discriminate. People with limited means and with resources can all be tempted or pressured to choose a credential they can't afford. Especially if is one that they hoped for and dreamed about. Postsecondary education is laden with emotional and economic pressures. It is unfortunate that so many options cost so much.

---

[10] Androitis, Brown, and Shifflett, "Families Go Deep in Debt to Stay in the Middle Class."

CHAPTER 6

Cash

cash: *the financial resources someone has*

The year 2019 was tough for our family. We faced several scary medical issues, and when December came, we were ready for a new year and fresh start. We were determined to make 2020 our best year yet. Little did we know that a bat in a meat market in Wuhan, China, was about to turn our lives upside down.

We were not prepared for a global pandemic. In January and February, our family looked to China with concern and sympathy, but safe distance. I kept traveling for work, dashing in and out of places like Seattle and New Orleans right before they became COVID-19 hotspots. And then March came, a fiercer and more frightening lion than any of us expected. Within weeks, hundreds of thousands were sick, domestic deaths were happening every 15 seconds, and more than 20 million adults had filed for unemployment. Many more—like my mom, who is a substitute teacher—suddenly found themselves in an economic purgatory, trying to file for cash assistance but unable to because of outdated online systems and maxed out phone lines.

The first weeks of COVID-19 typify—on a grand scale—the kinds of economic upheaval today's young people are growing up with and will continue to experience throughout their lives. Whether it is disruption sparked by pandemic, stock market, climate change, politics, or a combination, the volatility is getting more intense and frequent. And, as COVID-19 has taught us, these disruptions can last much longer than any of us expect or want.

Before COVID-19, America was experiencing historically low unemployment rates and healthy job growth. Pundits called our economy "red hot" and it felt like we had fully rebounded from the Wall Street–induced Great Recession. But once that bat got sick and the world got infected, everything changed. Suddenly, tens of millions of jobs were lost, and workers furloughed. The US became even more deeply divided along class and racial lines.

When schools and colleges initially closed, wealthier (and mostly white) young people and their families retreated to their homes—or vacation homes—with plenty of food and access to web-enabled digital devices; they were able to keep learning and working from the comfort of bedrooms and dining room tables. Many young people had well-educated parents at home, available to support them while working jobs that were able to convert into remote work.

On the other side of America's economic divide, some 20 million young people immediately lost access to free and reduced meals.[1] More than 100,000 had no homes to quarantine in.[2] These young people were not able to shelter and continue learning in place—instead, they tried to stay safe and keep up with schoolwork while bouncing around, from cars to overcrowded apartments, or temporary shelters.

In between America's wealthiest and poorest families were millions who were suddenly thrown into financial distress.

These cash-stretched and emotionally stressed households were not conducive for focused and rich learning or healthy youth development. The shift to crisis remote and distance learning was far from equal learning for all. Learning slowed, stalled, or even stopped for those without secure homes, sufficient food, reliable internet, or a digital device. Some schools in poorer communities just called it a day, deciding that learning could not continue under these conditions, and sending students home with printed review packets and ungraded busy work.

The initial weeks of COVID-19 highlight how economic loss leads to learning loss, and the next few years will illuminate how consequential those losses really are. Decades of research make it clear that this learning

---

[1] To give you a sense of how many kids this is, it is roughly equivalent to the population of Florida.

[2] Nikita Stewart, "She's 10, Homeless and Eager to Learn. But She Has No Internet," *The New York Times*, March 26, 2020, sec. New York. https://www.nytimes.com/2020/03/26/nyregion/new-york-homeless-students-coronavirus.html.

loss will lead to long-term personal and societal economic loss. As global and economic disruptions continue, our poorest families will be plunged deeper into poverty, and others into financially crisis.

Raised in Recessions

For older kids and young adults, the recession triggered by COVID-19 was not their first. The high school graduating class of 2020 was in kindergarten when the Great Recession hit. The major economic crises of our lifetime have bookended their K–12 experience, defining their childhoods and now their transitions into adulthood and the job market. When these young people entered school, many of their parents were losing jobs or struggling to pay the bills. Now these young people are graduating and worried about finding work and making enough money to get by.

Because of these life experiences, today's young people yearn for financial security and stability. They are less likely to take economic risks and—in a great American shift—value their financial stability over upward mobility. In spite of their hopes and apprehensions, they will work and raise families in a world that is not stable or secure.

Building Recession Resilience and Cash Savviness

When it comes to being ready for tomorrow's world, having competencies, connections, and credentials are critical. And yet, cash stands out as the true make-it-or-break-it currency. Without it, young people's ability to accrue the other currencies is greatly diminished. Each of us has a responsibility to care and plan for young people's financial stability and health.

Since we care about young people's learning and futures, let's establish three guiding principles for caring about their financial health:

1. We must support and keep young people learning during times of financial struggle, when they are barely getting by.
2. We must remove prohibitive cost barriers from educational and recreational opportunities, enabling access and the ability to level up.
3. We must help young people build the knowledge, skills, and resources they need to be financially aware and prepared.

Getting By

Having a newborn is exhausting. Those first few months feel like living in an alternate universe. For all the joy that babies bring, they come with prolonged sleep deprivation and incessant demands. In those early days, anything beyond the "sleep, feed, change, wash" baby cycle feels like too much to handle.

If you have cared for a newborn—or had other periods of sleepless nights and high demands—you know the feeling. Needing rest and feeling stressed are a killer combination.

Financial Distress plus the Rest and Stress Loop

When young people feel like they are just getting by—especially when they and their families are in financial distress—they can get stuck in survival mode; this initiates an endless feedback loop of distraction, stress, and exhaustion.[3]

- **We need rest** because it is when our brains and bodies are hard at work, repairing and restoring. Sleep and downtime are important parts of problem-solving and cognitive processing.[4] Years of research prove that in order to learn and work well, you need to be rested. Our resting brains organize the information we take in, make sense of it, and look to solve the problems we are confronting when we are awake.[5]
- Meanwhile, **stress is how our bodies try to protect us from threats.** Our stress response kicks in when we find ourselves in a scary situation or "stressing out" over challenges. This sends energy to our arms and legs (to fight or run from the threat) as well as the impulsive part of the brain (the amygdala). This extra energy is borrowed from the thinking part of the brain (the frontal lobe).

---

[3] Keith Payne, *The Broken Ladder: How Inequality Affects the Way We Think, Live, and Die* (Penguin Random House, 2017).
[4] Daniel J. Levitin, *Successful Aging: A Neuroscientist Explores the Power and Potential of Our Lives* (Penguin Random House, 2020).
[5] Alex Soojung-Kim Pang, *Rest* (Basic Books, 2016).

Cash scarcity and prolonged financial distress puts young people in chronic survival mode. This makes it harder to think and perform. It interferes with learning and work, as well as the ability to live a full, healthy life. Cash scarcity is not reserved for the poor. In fact, most American families experience significant financial unsteadiness each year. And very few American families have the savings to support them during periods of significant income loss.[6]

Cash Scarcity Limits Learning and Work

In 2013, *Science* published an article called *Poverty Impedes Cognitive Function*. In it, US behavioral economists Sendhil Mullainathan and Eldar Shafir, along with their Oxford-based colleague, Anandi Mani, alleged that a lack of cash leads to decision-making and cognitive performance. The researchers found that people who are poor are not worse decision makers or less smart than those who are wealthy, but rather, the act of being or feeling poor adversely effects decision-making and cognitive skills.

This was proven in a study of sugarcane farmers in Tamil Nadu, a state in southern India. Sugarcane farmers' incomes fluctuate according to the harvest. The researchers found that when farmers' incomes were low, they did far worse on tasks requiring focus and critical thinking. The research team was able to control for time, nutrition, and effort.

The conclusion, later explained in Sendhil and Eldar's book *Scarcity: Why Having Too Little Means So Much,* is that being poor or feeling poor is cognitively and emotionally taxing. It demands our time, commands and depletes our attention and focus, and pulls these limited resources away from other things, like learning and work.

Basically, being or feeling poor saps our mental energy, keeping attention on getting by, rather than learning new things or solving problems. It also makes us short-sighted—immediate demands eclipse the ability to look farther out and think about the future.[7] This can lead to risky behaviors and impulsive choices, born out of an urgent and biological need to get or do something right away.

---

[6] Jonathan Morduch and Rachel Schneider. *The Financial Diaries: How American Families Cope in a World of Uncertainty* (Princeton Press, 2017).
[7] Ibid.

Scarcity comes from being or feeling behind—behind in money, time, or other resources. Left unaddressed, it keeps getting worse, especially for young people. When today's kids struggle to pay attention, do their work, or behave, they may be having scarcity issues.

Behind from the Start

Kids born into poverty face more than scarcity issues. They also face systemic barriers to success. These young people start out behind wealthier peers. Their parents may not be able to afford to live in a safe neighborhood. They may not be able to access a quality early childhood center, or benefit from enriching extras, like "Mommy-and-Me" classes, community arts programs, or a YMCA membership. It is not that their parents want to deprive them; it is that their parents' own financial deprivation makes it impossible to afford or even consider how to make those extras possible.

As a result, many kids from lower-income homes start kindergarten behind in learning and language skills. They may experience developmental delays. It can be harder for these young people to sit still, pay attention, and learn what is being taught. It gets worse if they are also tired, hungry, or suffering from living conditions that strain relationships and health.

If these same kids end up attending underresourced schools—which often happens—things get even worse. When schools experience cash scarcity, they end up overcrowded, with inadequate or unsafe facilities; they experience teacher shortages, forced cuts to extracurricular programs, and insufficient resources and supplies.

Compounded and Collective Scarcity

This youth-in-environment scarcity is something I saw every day at my school. We had smart and talented kids who were years behind academically and developmentally. This did not reflect what we knew they were capable of. Instead, it reflected the limited opportunities and resources they had growing up.

Without intensive intervention and investments for them and their families, young people growing up poor risk entering adulthood far behind wealthier peers. Many will never be in a position to catch up. Unequal opportunities will follow them throughout their lives, and oftentimes, get passed on to their children.

No group suffers from this collective scarcity as much as young people of color who are poor. Black and brown families have historically been walled-off from economic opportunities and resources. As a whole, Native young people have experienced some of the most extreme poverty, economic isolation, and deprivation. Lines have been drawn through exclusionary practices that have kept people of color out of certain schools, jobs, and neighborhoods; or even from getting loans to start new businesses or buy a home. Across generations, this has meant that many Black and brown children live in communities that are severely underresourced, in families that struggle financially, and within a society that blames and punishes them for being so far behind.

Economic barriers to learning and development require our creativity, not defeat or excuse-making. We must be prepared help young people weather tough times and prepare them to get through those times. This takes a combination of kindness and understanding, solid supports and services, knowledge and skill-building.

How to Support Kids Who Struggle to Get By

While few of us can provide direct cash assistance to kids and families who need it, we can all put certain practices in place that will make life easier for young people who are financially distressed, to improve their ability to keep learning and developing. When kids are poor or feel poor, they will struggle to learn and work because their attention is being diverted elsewhere. Because of this, these practices are designed to either meet unmet needs, or help young people refocus their time and energy:

- **Lighten the Load.** Many high school students spend up to five hours each night on homework, and even more if they are in honors or AP classes. For younger kids, schedules may be overloaded with extracurriculars, sports, or other activities. Keeping up with all of that while also struggling financially is a recipe for burnout. To lighten the load for young people who are experiencing financial struggles, reduce deadlines and demands. Reduce quantity, not quality. Make deadlines flexible or combine tasks so there are fewer to keep track of. Cash scarcity will max out a young person's cognitive load, and you do not want to add to it unnecessarily. Help young people get things off their plates. Work to strengthen their *focus and get things done* competency. The ability to prioritize, focus, and keep track of things are effective antidotes to scarcity.

- **Put Maslow before Blooms.** When COVID-19 closed schools, my colleagues in Virginia encouraged educators to put "Maslow before Blooms." The idea was to meet basic needs before expecting young people to engage in cognitively demanding tasks. Schools and nonprofits are the center of communities and are well-positioned to provide everything from free meals to basic healthcare, cash assistance, mental health supports, and community connections. Educators can do amazing things to help kids and families financially. One middle school in a St. Louis gave students matched savings accounts. For every dollar saved, a dollar was matched to be applied to long-term savings. Even if you can't do big things, start out small. As a teacher, I always had a generous food stash and clean school uniforms in my desk drawers for students who needed them.
- **Upgrade Bandwidth.** We have all experienced bandwidth issues. Brains are somewhat similar to an internet connection. When there are too many things competing for attention, everything slows down and sometimes things stop working. Young people can improve their cognitive and emotional bandwidth by practicing mindfulness. Just like internet bandwidth, this is about learning what can be shut off, ignored, or temporarily paused. This is done through practicing focus and concentration, finding time to rest and recharge, and limiting distractions. This is about helping young people learn how to shift out of survival mode.
- **Engage Families.**[8] Economic hardship is rarely felt individually, especially for kids. They struggle to get by because their families struggle to get by. Maybe this is because a parent lost a job, or someone is sick. Maybe an unexpected expense cropped up. A family's financial situation can heighten anxiety and stress at home, sometimes contributing to child abuse or neglect. While we may not be able to stop or fix these issues, we can stick close to families, making it easier to know what is going on at home. That clearer picture of a young person's history, reality, and personal context can help us figure out what supports and services they need.

Getting Ahead

My colleague and her sister Sarah grew up in a rural, small town in the Northeast. Early on, their family worried something wasn't right

---

[8] My favorite family engagement expert is Dr. Steve Constantino. I got to know Steve when he led the Virginia Department of Education. Steve's book *Engage Every Family: Five Simple Principles* (Corwin, 2016) should be on every educator's bookshelf.

with Sarah. While other kids her age were talking, Sarah wasn't. Her parents raised concerns with teachers and the pediatrician. No one knew what to do. Eventually, Sarah was diagnosed with ADD. This entitled her to an IEP but even that did not come with the full range of supports she needed. In school, Sarah was different and disruptive enough to be labeled a behavior problem. Her teachers lacked the resources and training to deal with kids like her, who needed more personalized attention and support. Desperate to do something, her mom took a part-time job at the school. At least, then, she could keep an eye on her daughter.

Private schools and therapy were out of the question. Her family struggled financially, and the cost of private schooling or special services, especially given their rural location, was hard to consider or locate. And so, Sarah grew up in a community and in schools that were unable to provide the services and supports she needed. Her family's financial situation limited what was possible, and—in some cases—even knowing what was available.

Later in life, Sarah learned she had been misdiagnosed. She actually has Asperger syndrome, an autism spectrum disorder. What was seen as misbehavior was likely her need for structure, order, and routine. Her cash-strapped schools and ill-equipped (and probably poorly paid) teachers and therapists were not resourced to properly address her needs. The cumulative cost of those shortfalls has been significant.

Today, Sarah struggles to find and keep a job. Still living in her hometown, she is at least 30 minutes from an economic center. A while back, she got hired at the local grocery store, but it lasted less than a week.

Meanwhile, innovators in Silicon Valley and New York City are talking about the value of neurodivergent employees, workers like Sarah. Today, there are high-paying jobs well suited for her. She sees the world, picks up on patterns, and follows instructions in ways that are valuable and unique. With the right accommodations and supports, she could succeed in a high-wage career.

Companies like Goldman Sachs now run paid training programs to give neurodivergent job prospects, like Sarah, experience and exposure to their firms. These programs come with mentorship, skill-building, and professional development opportunities.[9] All of this makes me wonder

---

[9] Gwen Moran, "As Workers Become Harder to Find, Microsoft and Goldman Sachs Hope Neurodiverse Talent Can Be the Missing Piece," *Fortune*, December 7, 2019. https://fortune.com/2019/12/07/autism-aspergers-adhd-dyslexia-neurodiversity-hiring-jobs-work/

what Sarah's early adulthood and working life would have been like if she had grown up in a wealthier family and better-resourced community. Would she have been properly diagnosed early on, and more adequately served and supported throughout school? Could a change in financial status have opened up totally different opportunities, like regular and high-quality therapy, supports that could have positioned her for future jobs with employers like Goldman Sachs or Microsoft? Instead, Sarah struggles— along with so many like her—just to find and keep low-wage work.

Sarah's story is not one of capability but constraint. The adults in her life did the best they could with what they had. It still wasn't enough. Her family and community couldn't access or provide the advantages and opportunities—specialized classes, quality and sustained therapy, social and life skills training, supportive jobs—that would have set Sarah up for future economic success.

Glass Floors and Ceilings

In America, the best way to secure a great education and high-paying job is to have rich parents. Wealthy families pass down or purchase opportunity for their kids. They live in the best public school districts; enroll their kids in elite athletics or private music lessons; they can afford special services or therapy; and they send their kids to enriching summer camps and enroll them in other extracurriculars. These economic nudges push their children toward future merit-based scholarships and prime internships and jobs. According to my colleague Taylor Jo Isenberg, who runs the Economic Security Project, "Having expendable income leads to different life outcomes."

In 2017, Richard Reeves, a senior fellow at the Brookings Institution, proved why that is. In his book *Dream Hoarders: How the American Upper Middle Class Is Leaving Everyone Else in the Dust, Why That Is a Problem, and What to Do About It*, he describes an America that prides itself on the lore of being able to move from rags to riches, but actually operates by a reliable system of economic and social class reproduction. This means that if you are born poor in America, you have a good chance of staying poor throughout your life; and, if you are born rich, you will likely retain your financial security. This class reproduction doesn't care about talent, industry, or intelligence; it runs on opportunity.

The best way to get ahead in America is to be born ahead already.

As Richard explains, most of us are familiar with the "glass ceiling" that keeps people out of high-paying jobs and leadership positions—especially people of color and women. But that ceiling also functions as a less-acknowledged glass floor for those born into rich and resourced families.

Glass floors look like families using their economic means to ensure their kids grow up in affluent areas, attend the best schools, and seek out advantageous internships; glass floors are in effect whenever wealthy kids get into financial trouble and someone steps in to help before things get hard.[10]

Understand that smarts, grits, and talent only get you so far in America—what you really need is access and the ability to afford the right resources and opportunities. That is extremely easy for some, and nearly impossible for others.

The Cost of a Free Education

As I talked about this issue of cash and opportunity with my friend, Chris Jones—a high school principal in Virginia—he brought up how many hidden costs there are in a free, public education. I was so struck by his laundry list of expenses, that I went home and looked it up.

Chris was right. Each year, Communities in Schools partners with Huntington Bank to calculate household spending on school supplies and related fees. According to their annual Backpack Index, here are estimates of what families with kids in public school paid in 2019:

- $1,017 for every elementary school student
- $1,277 for every middle school student
- $1,668 for every high school student[11]

---

[10] Some researchers I rely on for information on the intersection of *poverty and opportunity* are Jason Purnell, Mark Rank, Raj Chetty, Richard Reeves, and Robert Putnam.

[11] "Huntington's 13th Annual Backpack Index Spotlights the Role of Technology in Rising Back-to-School Costs," *Communities in Schools*, July 18, 2019. https://www.communitiesinschools.org/press-room/resource/huntingtons-13th-annual-backpack-index-spotlights-role-technology-rising-back-school-costs/?utm_source=socialmedia&utm_medium=twitter&utm_campaign=backpackindex&utm_content=organic.

If my four siblings and I were in school today, my parents would have paid roughly $8,000 each year just to cover back-to-school costs. Not to mention any extra athletic and activity fees, contributions to the Booster Club or PTO, paying for uniforms or productions, after-school clubs, or travel costs to games and band concerts. Today, a family of four living at or below the poverty line can expect to spend at least one-third of their annual income on public school expenses.[12]

Unfortunately, many families aren't in a position to shell out an extra $1,000, let alone $10,000 in basic fees. Now consider the additional and sometimes astronomical costs for sports, activities, vacations, or a private school education.[13] For kids who grow up poor, many can expect that when they are old enough, their "free time" will be spent at a part-time or summer job to help cover household expenses. In these situations, there is not enough time or money for anything extra.

Opportunity Hoarding

It is easy to see how private school students unintentionally hoard opportunities from many public school students. But it is harder to admit how much of that goes on in our free, public schools. It occurs at two levels. There is the glass floor level, which are public schools in affluent areas. Schools tend to be funded by a formula tied to local property taxes; higher property values lead to more school funding. As a result, schools in wealthy communities can usually afford to offer many of the same opportunities as private schools. When they can't, families can generally make up the difference.

Then you have schools at the other end of the local tax base. These schools can't afford any extra expenses, forcing them to cut the arts and music, sports and field trips, and important upgrades to technology and equipment. Sometimes they even have to cut staff and student services. These schools overwhelmingly serve youth of color and those who are

---

[12] According to the US Department of Health and Human Services, the 2020 poverty guidelines say that a family of four is living in poverty if the annual household income is $26,200 or less.

[13] Suzanne Woolley and Katya Kazakina, "At $50,000 a Year, the Road to Yale Starts at Age 5," *Bloomberg*, March 27, 2019. https://www.bloomberg.com/news/articles/2019-03-27/at-50-000-a-year-baby-ivies-road-to-yale-starts-at-age-5.

poor. This only exacerbates the opportunity gaps these young people already experience.

In between, you have average American public schools—like Chris's. They pay for what they can, but still need families to contribute a little more each year. In these schools, students who struggle financially are often no better off than if they attended an underresourced school. Without being able to pay for activities and fees out-of-pocket, they can't participate in the essential extras.

The Cost of Getting into College and Careers

There are also hidden costs associated with getting into college, finding an internship, or starting a job that leads to a career. This was flagrantly broadcast in 2018, when celebrities, including Lori Loughlin (known as "Becky" in *Full House* to most of us) and Felicity Huffman ("Lynette" in *Desperate Housewives*), along with 50 others, were charged in a scheme to get their kids into prestigious universities.

As if the cost of college was not high enough, these families shelled out tens of millions of dollars to William Singer to bribe, barter, forge, and falsify records, all to get their kids into top colleges. Singer hired people to take and ace the SAT/ACT for his client's children; he created false records of athletic accomplishments and paid off university coaches to get these young people admitted.[14]

This scandal demonstrated how far some families will go to guarantee their children's future education and economic success. There are millions of less-scandalous families with similar ambitions who are willing to pay thousands of dollars (which they sometimes have to borrow) to college prep tutors and companies to raise their children's test scores and try to improve their chances of getting into college.

For young people who can't afford scholarship-worthy extracurriculars and honors classes and then can't afford college-prep services, the odds of getting into top colleges are stacked against them.

---

[14] Jennifer Medina, Katie Benner, and Kate Taylor, "College Admissions Scandal: Actresses, Business Leaders and Other Wealthy Parents Charged," *The New York Times*, March 12, 2019. https://www.nytimes.com/2019/03/12/us/college-admissions-cheating-scandal.html.

Taking an Economic Hit to Jump-Start
Your Career

When young people are ready to find their first job, there are those who have enough savings or family financial assistance to take an unpaid or low-paid opportunity because it feels like the right strategic move.

This is a privileged and less exposed path to prosperity in America. It includes going to college and then spending college breaks at unpaid internships or in entry-level positions that foster important professional connections ("door openers"), that end up jump-starting your career. Those who can afford to do this are commonly the ones who are already ahead.

To equal the playing field, schools should seek out paid work-based learning opportunities for their students; employers should only offer paid internships, and should also put applicants through a review process that deliberately seeks to reduce bias and preferential treatment.

Economic Transport on America's Opportunity Pathways

All in all, getting ahead in America is a bit like trying to get around in Los Angeles traffic.

There are those without transportation or money to ride the bus, call a cab, or use a ride share service. For them, opportunities are limited to whatever is walkable. Then there are those with enough money for public transit or an occasional ride share, but not enough to own their own vehicle. For them, there are more opportunities, but with certain stops and limited routes. They can only go so far.

There are those who own a vehicle and can get around but have to compete with LA traffic—subject to traffic jams and roadblocks along the way. Then there are others who hitch a ride with a friend or family member, able to benefit from the HOV lane and someone else's toll pass, leading to a faster ride with fewer stops and less traffic.

And finally, there are the super wealthy—not only do they have a vehicle and toll pass, but they can also afford to use the helicopter path when they need to. This enables them to fly over traffic and roadblocks, with air traffic control clearing the path to their destination.

One aspect of helping young people make it in adulthood is being honest with them about what opportunity pathways are now open and available to them, as well as what type of economic transport they have or need. If you can help them upgrade their economic transportation options, that's great. And if you can't, then try and bring new opportunities to them.

How to Reduce or Remove Hidden Opportunity Costs

- **Whenever and However You Can, Provide Direct Cash Assistance to Kids and Families Who Need It.** A life of struggle is costly, and a life of opportunities expensive. For kids who qualify for government financial assistance, make sure they have the tools to apply and receive benefits. Go farther by investigating basic income pilot programs,[15] Individual Development Account (IDA) options, and other cash assistance and asset-building opportunities that they may qualify for. Not sure where to start? Consider checking in with your local banks, or a nearby Federal Reserve.
- **Advocate for Public Funding That Supports Students' Back-to School and Activity Costs**. Get together with educators, parents, and community members and approach your local school board, city council, state education department, or elected officials to appeal for more public funding to cover student supply costs and participation fees.
- **Waive Fees or Apply Sliding Scales for Extracurricular and Enrichment Activities**. These programs and activities benefit young people in so many ways, especially by building the competencies and connections they will need throughout life. A young person's financial status should not prevent participation. If you must charge, consider a sliding scale, scholarships, and waiving fees for families under a certain income level.
- **Make Quality College and Credential Planning Free and Available for All Young People.** Until every credentialing provider decides to overhaul their admissions criteria and forgo college entrance exams, every young person should benefit from the preparatory and planning services that help them to compete in the college admissions process.
- **Grow Young People's Social Capital to Increase Their Future Earnings Potential.** Consider creative ways to build young people's connections by expanding their opportunities and network. There is a strong link between cash and connections. Kids need door openers—or, as the case may be, ceiling openers.

---

[15] For more on basic income, check out the Economic Security Project, or *Fair Shot: Rethinking Inequality and How We Earn* (2018), which is written by ESP co-founder, Chris Hughes.

Smoothing Out

When I was a school leader, I was confused by our state's high school financial literacy requirement. At that time, it could be satisfied by passing a fairly simple multiple-choice test. As I recall, it covered just the basics, and—as with many tests—the content was quickly forgotten after the test was taken. I worried that my students' required financial literacy did nothing to equip them for their financial realities.

Those realities have been well-documented by researchers Jonathan Morduch and Rachel Schneider. They followed 235 low- and middle-income families for more than a year to better understand the regular financial ups and downs American families face. What they found was very different from what normally gets taught in school.

Here are the basic financial life cycle principles taught in a typical US financial literacy course or class:

- Save slowly and steadily across your lifetime, ideally starting with a college fund set up in childhood.
- Get a job with benefits, including retirement, and try to save more money each year.
- Make smart investments whenever you can.
- Pay off your debts and enjoy asset ownership (e.g., own your car and house).
- Retire comfortably.
- Have enough money saved to support your children and give them a better financial life than you had.

According to Jonathan and Rachel, these principles assume that most people follow this trajectory, and that with enough financial literacy, discipline, and budgeting, people can live a financially stable or prosperous life.[16]

Meanwhile, Jonathan and Rachel found that the financial realities for most Americans tell a very different story.

---

[16] Morduch and Schneider. *The Financial Diaries: How American Families Cope in a World of Uncertainty.*

- Most adults experience regular spikes and dips in income, leading to monthly and yearly income volatility.
- Income dips can quickly spiral into serious financial stress, depleting savings, and ushering in periods of true financial struggle.
- Many adults have little to no savings, including for retirement. In fact, most adults cannot come up with a few hundred dollars to cover an unexpected expense.
- Financial insecurity—or feeling like you only have enough to get by—is found at every income level.

In addition to doing what we can to help young people get by and get ahead, we also need to do what we can to prepare them for their financial futures. This can be tricky, because not all of us feel particularly cash-savvy ourselves. Especially lately. The economic ups and downs we have collectively experienced have taken a personal toll on many of us, one that few of our financial plans have withstood.

There is a new financial life cycle emerging, and young people need to learn how to manage within it. It is built on the premise that most if not all of us will experience financial "precarity" over our lifetimes. The poorest will be hardest hit.

Financial precarity is the experience of routine financial stress and struggle because of insufficient wages, not enough savings, and bad luck (for example, financial stress brought on by an unexpected global pandemic).[17]

Yesterday's Financial Cycle	*Tomorrow's Financial Cycle*
Slow and steady savings over time.	Savings used for spending spikes and financial emergencies.
Building investments and retirement savings over a career.	Periodic and significant dips in investments and benefits contributions.
Retirement in your 50s or 60s, financed by social security, a pension, or retirement savings.	Needing to work into your 70s or 80s, with variable retirement income options.

(*Continued*)

[17] Carrie Leana, "The Cost of Financial Precarity," *Stanford Social Innovation Review*, Spring 2019.

Yesterday's Financial Cycle	Tomorrow's Financial Cycle
Relative economic stability with employment.	Anticipated month-to-month financial ups and downs.
Upward economic mobility where earnings and savings go up over time.	Multiple stages of life in different earnings brackets. More frequent rotations of financial security and instability.
The inability to save and meet expenses is due to poor budgeting and financial planning.	Economic volatility begets more volatility. It is easy to financially spiral once you are hit by a significant or unexpected expense. These "spending shocks" are happening often.
Strive for financial prosperity.	Strive for financial stability and security.

It is time to convert our financial literacy courses into longer-term learning experiences focused on financial agility and resourcefulness—equipping young people with the tools and skills they need to weather a lifetime of financial difficulties. According to Jonathan and Rachel, the key is finding ways to stay "financially smooth" over time.

Being financially smooth requires cash strategies and coping skills. Young people need strategies for managing and minimizing financial volatility and coping with financial ups and downs. This requires some degree of financial competence, cash savings, and social connections to turn to for support and assistance.

Before becoming financially independent, young people should be able to set and pursue short-term savings goals and plan for financial emergencies and unforeseen expenses. They will need as much education on taxes, borrowing, and debt management as they get on savings and investments. They must also know who or where to turn to for financial assistance in a crisis. Ideally, they should have healthy and reliable people or institutions who can share financial resources during times of need.

Moving from practical matters to emotional ones, financial precarity does a number on our mental health. By understanding that financial precarity is common, we can help young people prepare for the possibility by supporting the development of healthy coping skills, such as being able to calm down, stay healthy and optimistic, and keep perspective.

A quick one-credit course, three-day program, or exam at the end of high school is woefully insufficient for preparing today's kids for the financial realities of tomorrow's world. Cash management and preparing young people to stay financially smooth needs to become a learning and preparatory thread that follows young people from childhood into adulthood.

HOW TO IMPROVE YOUNG PEOPLE'S FINANCIAL EDUCATION

- **Start Early and Don't Stop.** To be prepared for their financial futures, today's kids need cash strategies and coping skills. That includes strong money sense in addition to competencies that are best developed early in life. Consider starting young people's financial education in childhood and keep it going through the transition into adulthood.
- **Focus Financial Education on Becoming Financially Smooth.** Assume that most young people will experience financial precarity. To be ready, they will need to learn about savings and investing, as well as borrowing and managing debt.
- **Move from Exam to Experience.** Young people need tools, strategies, and tips to use in adulthood. Make financial education an experiential and active learning experience.
- **Provide Social and Emotional Support.** Financial health is connected to the ability to cope and get support during financially tough times. Consider social-emotional learning as a part of young people's overall financial education.

PART III
Currency-Building

Chapter 7: Becoming a Currency-Builder

CHAPTER 7

Becoming a Currency-Builder

As educators—of all kinds—our job is to meet young people's needs, support their growth and development, and prepare them for life. We have fulfilled this responsibility if young people are able to enter adulthood with the knowledge, skills, and supports they need to get started, along with the resourcefulness to get what they need down the road.

This work continues even when the future feels unpredictable. During these times, it is critical that we get a handle on what is happening, so that we can anticipate the full range of young people's possible futures, and figure out what those possibilities require. The stakes are high, and lives are on the line. We cannot afford to operate from outdated notions of what readiness used to require.

In Pursuit of Long, Livable Lives

In 2017, the World Economic Forum published a white paper called *We'll Live to 100—How Can We Afford It?* In it, WEF noted the rapid increase in life expectancy—noting that babies born in 2017 can expect to live to at least 2117. This is because many previously lethal conditions are now treatable, and with our quickly growing aging population, more resources are being poured into finding ways to delay, reduce, or get rid of the ailments of old age.

Today's kids should be prepared for the possibility of a 100-year life. Our job is not finished with a handoff at 18 to a college, employer, or the United States military. Instead, it should be viewed as a partnership with young people throughout the first quarter of their lives, to support them in getting what they need to make it during the next three quarters. We are preparing young people for the possibility of a 100-year life.

We must expand our visions and missions beyond college- and career-readiness and set a new bar.

The goal should be a long, livable life. We are preparing young people to keep living, learning, and working across many years of opportunity and hardship, significant change and innovation. When we expand our view of education beyond content, to include currencies, we up the chances that today's kids will make it over the long haul.

Currency-Building for a Livable Life

In 2005, Dan Buettner—a travel writer and modern-day explorer—wrote a cover story for *National Geographic* on "The Secrets of a Long Life." In the article, he explored the characteristics of three communities with some of the world's healthiest, longest-lived people. These communities were dubbed "Blue Zones" for the alleged blue ink pens the research team used to write field notes. Buettner, along with a team of demographers, medical scientists, and journalists, found that although these communities were different, they shared certain similarities in lifestyle and diet. These longevity hotspots ranged from the coastal community of Okinawa, Japan; to the mountainous villages of remote Sardinia, Italy; to the Seventh Day Adventists in urban Loma Linda, California.

Now, imagine the year is 2100. We are entering a new century and at least half of today's kids are 100 or older. A social researcher—maybe Buettner's great granddaughter is traveling with her team to places with the greatest numbers of centenarians. She wants to better understand those shared qualities among them, and the places where they grew up.

Before setting out, she studies communities where people have the shortest lifespans. Here she finds rampant systemic and racial inequality and what future social scientists might dub "opportunity deserts." In these communities, predominantly Black and brown, the first quarter of life is marked by insufficient learning and work options, financial struggle, and personal challenge. The education and training systems in these places are largely as they were a century or two before, more outdated each year, preparing young people for lives and jobs that no longer exist.

With this picture in mind, the research team embarks on a journey to communities with well-lived 100-year-olds. Centenarian interviews likely reveal the many options and opportunities these individuals experienced growing up. Their learning and development probably occurred in-person and online, and across a connected network of places—at school, in the community, at home, and even in work-based settings. They recall their communities as the classroom, and their educators as a diverse group of adults who always sought to better understand them and the world around them.

Each centenarian tells the research team a different story, but I imagine all describe the many different ways they were able to develop the competencies they needed throughout life; the connections that supported and assisted them along the way; the credentials that validated what they knew and could do; and the cash to not only get by but to get ahead.

The interviewers ask each centenarian to talk about the adults who supported their learning and development. The stories would certainly differ, but I bet a set of common characteristics would emerge. Based on the research and all we have explored so far, here is what I imagine those five "currency-builder" characteristics would be:

1. Take a whole-person, whole-life approach.
2. Make currencies a part of every learning experience.
3. Build currencies wherever young people spent time.
4. Be just, inclusive, and caring.
5. Be advocates and allies.

You can be the currency-builder that our young people need today. All it takes is elevating and integrating the currencies into whatever you are already doing. There are no new models to adopt or prescriptive reforms to put in place. Currency-building can live alongside anything. On the front-end, this only requires willingness, creative planning, and the commitment to provide the space and time for young people to be themselves, to practice and play.

The challenge to become a currency-builder starts with believing that every kid is entitled to make it in adulthood and experience a 100-year livable life.

From there, you will need to figure out if your actions match this belief. Try to examine your behaviors and biases and evaluate your relationships and practices. This requires a commitment to antiracism and to use whatever privilege you have to address injustice when you see it. It also requires a posture of continuous personal learning and development.

If your actions match this belief, give yourself permission to prioritize currencies and young people's needs, even if you work in a system or school that tends to prioritize completion and systems compliance.

You will probably move faster than schools or organizations can. Systems change takes time. Acknowledge this and move on. Young people can't wait for systems to catch up. And you don't have to wait, either. Today's kids need you and a whole community of currency-builders behind them, supporting them, and ensuring they have everything they need to make it in tomorrow's world.

Currency-Builder Characteristic #1: Take a Whole-Person, Whole-Life Approach

To make it and achieve a long, livable life, young people will need to be ready to continuously learn, work, and grow. Learning, working, and personal change are all more powerful and positive when we are okay mentally, physically, emotionally, and socially. If one aspect of life is out of balance, everything is.

Focus on the Whole Person

A whole-person approach invites us to see young people for who they are, what they want and need, as well as the histories and environments they come from. As a currency-builder, we should customize and contextualize accordingly.

Consider the growth charts that pediatricians use to track how kids grow and develop. After asking questions and taking certain measurements, a child is charted according to typical standards, as well as their own trajectory. Based on where they land and the other factors in their lives, the pediatrician personalizes recommendations for what can be done to support the young person's healthy growth and development. It is very much the same with the currencies.

Here are some measurements—or dimensions—of a whole life to keep track of as you support young people and help them get ready for what's ahead:[1]

Personal	Environmental
Cognitive	Economic and social status
Cultural	Family and friends
Emotional	Racial and cultural dynamics
Physical	Neighborhood or community climate
Social	Structural limitations or assets

A currency-builder keeps young people and their futures at the center of decision-making, always assessing how they are doing as a learner and in life, while keeping an eye on what they will need later on. This active and ongoing appraisal will enable you to adjust which currencies get focused on and why.

In concrete terms, consider a young person who struggles to make friends at school, but has already been accepted into college with a full scholarship. A currency-builder might focus more on building connections than credentials. Or, think about a young person who lives in poverty, but has a vibrant network of friends and family; the currency-builder might focus more on cash and less on connections.

At a community level, you can look across a group and find their shared interests, challenges, opportunities, and needs. Maybe you work at

---

[1] For more on this, I recommend reading, *Toward a Livable Life: A 21st Century Agenda for Social Work, The Promise of Adolescence: Realizing Opportunity for All* (National Academies Press, 2020).

a school and notice that counselors have been seeing an uptick in anxiety among students. In this case, it might be time to bolster competencies and connections that support mental health.

Or perhaps you are working with a young person who doesn't know if college is the right choice, or which credentials to look at. In this case, it might be time to focus on credentials, while simultaneously strengthening the competencies, connections, and cash that will assist in the overall credentialing process.

When we consider everything about a young person's life, we embrace the belief that learning and living are linked, and that as the adults that support their learning and development, we care about both.

Focus on the Whole Life

While a *whole-person* approach requires a broad perspective—keeping an expanded view of what a young person needs to learn and develop—a *whole-life* approach requires a long perspective—always striving to better enable and equip a young person for a long, livable life.

Let's stop talking about education pipelines and start talking about young people's lifetimes. The currency-building and learning opportunities in the first quarter of life make the next three quarters possible. And whatever is happening during that first quarter of life, dictates what economic realities are waiting for young people in adulthood.

A whole-life perspective also obligates currency-builders to fight and advocate for every young person to have the promise and possibility of a 100-year life in the first place. Babies born in places like Flint, Michigan, or the North Side of St. Louis city—both predominantly poor and Black—may die up to 20 years earlier than their wealthier and whiter peers, just because of where they are raised.[2] Issues of structural racism and social

---

[2] Mona Hanna-Attisha, "I'm Sick of Asking Children to Be Resilient," *The New York Times*, May 12, 2020, sec. Opinion. https://www.nytimes.com/2020/05/12/opinion/flint-inequality-race-coronavirus.html; Health Equity Works, *For the Sake of All: A Report on the Health and Well-Being of African Americans in St. Louis and Why It Matters for Everyone* (Washington University in St. Louis, 2015), https://healthequityworks.wustl.edu/items/for-the-sake-of-all-a-report-on-the-health-and-well-being-of-african-americans-in-st-louis-and-why-it-matters-for-everyone/

determinants of health—terms that might feel politicized or academic—are fundamental for currency-builders, requiring considerable attention, study, personal reflection, and action.

To be a currency-builder who adopts a whole-person and whole-life approach, you must see your role as one that extends beyond young people's learning to include their living and longevity. Today's kids will learn better if they are living with what they need. They will live better lives later on, if they benefited from rich learning opportunities and supports growing up.

Currency-Builder Characteristic #2: Make Currencies a Part of Every Learning Experience

Schools, programs, and families put this currency-builder characteristic into practice every day. Whenever a teacher gives students a group project that requires them to work together, apply learning, and be creative, they are building competencies and connections. Each time a counselor, mentor, or parent sits down with a young person to hear about what they want to do after graduation or to ask how things are going at home, they embrace a holistic perspective and question-asking stance that builds connections and guides a young person toward the right credentials and future economic opportunities. Every leadership decision to continue scholarships, remove cumbersome fees, and balance budgets in ways that protect young people's needs is a moment when cash is being built and more competency- and connection-building opportunities are being made available. In recent years, some models and approaches to teaching and learning have emerged that are especially currency-rich when implemented well.

If you are trying to find an organization, school, program, or model aligned to this currency-building approach, here are some key words to look for:

- Deeper learning
- Student-centered learning
- Positive youth development
- Project-, problem-, or inquiry-based learning
- social-emotional learning
- Work-based learning or "learn and earn" opportunities

I have found currency-builders in the Hampton City Schools in Virginia. Their training program for future EMTs builds all four currencies at once. Young people work with local first responders to practice being dispatchers. Doing this develops and demands competencies, nurtures new connections, leads to credential possibilities, and elevates future job and earnings potential (cash).

I have also found currency-builders a few hours west of Hampton, in Cumberland County, where students tinker away in a MakerSpace that includes 3D printers, robotics, and more. As they play and create, students of all ages strengthen competencies, while building critical connections with each other and machines—all of this while designing the kinds of things that will glow on a future credential or job application. In the MakerSpace, Cumberland students are encouraged to collaborate, innovate, and create. This past year, students built robot vacuums, lawnmowers, cell phone cases, and farmbots to support their agricultural community.

For those of us trained in the "plan with the end in mind" approach championed by the late, great, and deeply missed Grant Wiggins,[3] this currency-building characteristic is the ultimate backward-planning practice. In order for young people to be ready for the future, they need to be able to make it in this crazy, changing world. To make it, they need currencies. Therefore, we should design every learning experience as an opportunity to build currencies, ensuring that they transfer into the real world.

For school leaders and district or program administrators, this might run counter to some aspects of more compliance- and completion-oriented systems. As you set policy, design professional development for your staff, and establish annual learning targets and benchmarks, look for ways to braid and blend the four currencies into everyday interactions and mandated experiences.

---

[3] If you haven't read Grant Wiggins's work, now is the time! He and Jay McTighe wrote a number of books about "Understanding by Design." I was very fortunate to be mentored by Grant, who passed away in 2015. During our conversations, he would always remind me to focus on whatever is most important in a kid's life and then do everything within my power to get each kid there.

Currency-Builder Characteristic #3:
Build Currencies Wherever Learning Happens

Currency-building is not limited to the schoolhouse and classroom. It can happen whenever and wherever. And, when it does, it should always count. Today's kids will build competencies and connections, plan for future credentials, and work on their financial health at school, home, in sports, or theaters, before or after school, during summer or school breaks, in-person and online.

As currency-builders, we need to really familiarize ourselves with the spaces and places where young people spend time. Then, we should see how young people's network of people and places might work together to help them to learn, develop, and grow. Similar to a whole-person and whole-life perspective, this characteristic asks us to adopt a whole community approach.

Today's schools were not designed for tomorrow's world or for every kid. As currency-builders you will find yourself moving faster than systems and schools can. By working together—as a currency-building ecosystem—we can provide young people with the ongoing and continuous, equitable support and development they need, and we can share and distribute the load and available resources with one another.

If you want to learn more about putting this characteristic into practice, here are some key words to jump-start your search:

- Children's cabinets
- Community schools
- Community–school partnerships
- Education–employer partnerships
- Employer advisories or councils
- Family engagement
- P20 councils

When COVID-19 first closed our schools, we reeled in sudden awareness of how important strong partnerships are. This includes those between teachers and parents, community organizations and schools, employers and educators, just to name a few. We also saw how important it is for young people to be able to learn, wherever they are, and to be able to seamlessly transition from in-person to online, and then back again.

Currency-building requires places and people to work together to build a community-wide learning and youth readiness infrastructure and ecosystem. For younger kids, this requires a school-family-community base, and for older youth it is a school-family-community-work base. This infrastructure must be tech-enabled, broadband connected, and freely available to every single young person.

Within this currency-building ecosystem, the individual settings should be places that encourage and enable quality learning and positive youth development.

When I co-led *The Readiness Project* at the Forum for Youth Investment, we researched what these spaces and places look like. This is what we found:

- The learning **environment** should be welcoming, safe, and structured. It is a positive place where young people want to spend time, know what to expect, and know what is expected of them.
- The **relationships** should be authentic, positive, and productive. Adults and peers are caring, motivating, equipping, and empowering.
- The **experiences and opportunities** should keep young people challenged and engaged. Experiences and opportunities connect with young people based on who they are, where they are, what they need, and what they want.
- The environment affords young people **space and time** to learn, develop, and strengthen their currencies. This includes opportunities to practice and learn from mistakes, apply and connect, reflect, and continuously improve.

Currency-Builder Characteristic #4: Be Just, Inclusive, and Caring

Currency-builders should seek to listen to young people, learn from and about them, express empathy, and pursue equity. This means living out the belief that every kid deserves a long, livable life. Currency-builder characteristics #4 and 5 come as a pair. This is because *"being just, inclusive, and caring"* asks us to view readiness as a right, and *"being an advocate and ally"* compels us to act on that belief.

As currency-builders, we need to believe with our whole hearts that readiness is a basic human right and acknowledge that there are young people for whom this right isn't realized because of risks and barriers that are out of their control.

Schools and programs who understand this inequity, and are working to fix it, often commit to these practices:

- Antiracist education
- Cultural responsiveness
- Education justice
- Healing-centered practices
- Restorative justice
- Universal design

Being *just* is opening up the doors of opportunity that have been historically and commonly closed to young people because of who they are, where they live, or what they can afford. For example, in the chapter on cash, we explored what Richard Reeves calls the "glass floor." This is when young people born into wealth benefit from unearned privileges, like going to great schools or being selected for competitive internships because they know someone or can afford it while others cannot. Justice asks us to learn about how privilege and power works, use whatever privilege and power we have to call out injustice, and then do what we can to distribute opportunity and advantage.

Being *inclusive* invites us to create spaces where young people can see themselves, be themselves, and know they belong. This invites us to reflect young people's cultures and identities in everything from assignments and activities, to the pictures they see on the walls and characters they read about in books. Being themselves requires us to get to know our young people—where they come from, what they like and need—and then to create an environment that respects who and where they are in life.

Being *caring* is about empathy. The active cultivation and expression of empathy can help us get to equity. We should seek to understand what it is like to be the young people in our lives. If you have never been poor, it is hard to understand the complex stress of poverty; if you are white, it is easy to minimize the harms of racial profiling. If you have never struggled with a disability, it is easy to assign activities without considering accommodations. And the list goes on.

The best way to cultivate empathy is through close and loving relationships with people who are different from you. Sometimes this isn't possible. In that case, read, try to watch, and listen to stories—not just the news, but engrossing personal and fictional accounts—that allow you to enter into someone else's perspective, experiences, and thinking. This will build a better understanding of who different people are and how they experience the world.

Being *just, inclusive, and caring* means that currency-builders seek to stay humble, keep listening and learning, and remain open to changing beliefs and behaviors.

It also requires that we seek to build and back away—creating spaces where young people can be authentic agents of their own learning and development. This is a characteristic of practice and perspective, which invites a radical and regular examination of what we believe and who we may unintentionally be holding back, keeping out, or leaving behind. Beyond examination, it asks for our courage and honest change.

Currency-Builder Characteristic #5: Be an Advocate and Ally

Currency-builders are agents of change. When we see a wrong, we try to right it. This characteristic is about removing barriers, shifting power, and changing policies and structures, so that young people who are being held back can keep going, catch up, get ahead, and make it in adulthood. Occasionally, this requires stepping out of our comfort zones, being brave, and doing new things. This might mean writing a letter to the paper, speaking at a public meeting, contacting elected officials, or striking up a relationship with someone in an influential leadership position.

Effective advocates and allies know their issues, can tell compelling and personal stories that reflect the need for change, and have a list of specific and actionable demands. As currency-builders, our "special interest" is our young people and their readiness for life. We should find them platforms to share their own stories. When we can't or they don't want to, we should respectfully and carefully elevate their experiences, keeping their needs at the center of our demands. We must fight hardest for young people who are struggling the most. These young people can benefit the most from our advocacy efforts and assistance.

There are different ways to advocate and ally. You can spread ideas and engage in a movement, organize, lobby or petition, or even run for office.

Strategy	Description
Spread Ideas	Take advantage of social media and its virality. Pictures and stories shared through these platforms, such as Facebook, Instagram, and Twitter, can be a very effective advocacy tactic.[4] If you see an issue that you think others will identify with and be compelled to share, consider spreading your stories and demands online. This can be done through posts, videos, photos, or petitions.
Join a Movement	From #MeToo to #BlackLivesMatter to #BringTheGirlsBack, recent years have shown the enduring strength of protests and sit-ins, matched with new tactics, including Twitter hashtags and online campaigns. Another way to get active is to join organizers and groups who represent the issues your young people are being impacted by. Then make those demands your own. One well-known model for this is Everytown for Gun Safety and their local *Moms Demand Action* chapters. This advocacy model brings together professional organizers and regular people, in this case fighting to keep schools and kids safe from gun violence. If you don't have time to attend meetings, consider donating money.

[4] Jeremy Heimans and Henry Timms, *New Power: How Power Works in Our Hyperconnected World—and How to Make It Work for You* (Penguin Random House, 2018).

Strategy	Description
Petition or Lobby	Many young people are held back from the currencies they need because of persistent system and structural barriers. There are public rules and policies that often get in the way of progress. For currency-building, this might include local district policies for grade promotion or graduation requirements, which often rely too heavily on attendance and seat-time requirements. It can be school funding formulas, often outdated and complicated, that base education resourcing on local tax bases, ensuring poor communities end up with the fewest resources. It can also be federal policy, which determines who qualifies for assistance during periods of financial struggle. If you become aware of harmful policies and related practices, reach out to state and system leaders or elected officials (or become one), building rapport and relationship, and invite them to ally with you for change. If they refuse to ally, then apply persistent, nagging pressure through phone calls, visits, and notes. You can also do this through membership groups you already belong to—for example, a superintendent could join the policy and advocacy working group of her state superintendents' association.

Currency-builder advocates and allies look to make a positive and lasting difference in the lives of today's kids and their future world.[5] They commit to shift and distribute power, creating spaces and opportunities for young people to be their own best advocates, making sure that decisions about them are not made without them. Currency-builder advocates and allies do everything they can to understand young people's world as it is, and to fight for the world as it should be.[6]

---

[5] Tim Stafford, *Shaking the System: What I Learned from the Great American Reform Movements* (IVP Books, 2007).
[6] Edward T. Chambers, *Roots for Radicals: Organizing for Power, Action, and Justice* (The Continuum International Publishing Group, 2006).

Taking It to the Next Level

Readiness for tomorrow's world should be the right of every young person in America. Living life in tomorrow's world will be costly and require so much more than earning a high school diploma or college degree. Young people will rely on various kinds and combinations of competencies to live, work, and learn. They will need the credibility that comes with credentials to prove and validate what they know and can do. They will need substantial social and financial capital to afford the expenses and experiences that come with the possibility of a 100-year life. And, they will need to endure a world and time that is shaky and shifting, sometimes feeling as though it is spinning out of control.

This book was only about making it. Establishing the necessary baseline for getting started in adulthood, in a world that remains unfair and unjust. Without this, young people will find themselves constantly catching up and falling behind, especially those who started out behind by no fault of their own.

There is also an important difference between having the currencies to make it in life and having the enduring assets to thrive, enjoy life, and take it to the next level.

As currency-builders, the work described in this book is only the beginning. We start by helping today's kids acquire the currencies they need. As we do that, we must find other currency-builders and work collectively to change the world, systems and structures they are growing up in, finally making them fair and just. Currency-builders see this dual-role as a moral imperative.

Beyond making it, young people need us to help them flourish in changing and challenging times. To take whatever life looks like, and make it something worthwhile, meaningful, and healthful—to not just prepare, but provide today's kids with the promise of well-being and well-becoming.

ACKNOWLEDGMENTS

There have been so many people who contributed their time and smart thinking to this book.

First, I owe tremendous thanks to my mom and husband. My mom has worked in education for decades and my husband works with youth-serving leaders in East St. Louis. Each reflect different segments of *Making It's* audience, and both graciously agreed to be my first readers and editors. They also took care of the boys when I needed time to write. And thanks to my professional editing team at Jossey-Bass/Wiley, especially Kim Wimpsett, Cheryl Ferguson, Amy Fandrei, and Pete Gaughan.

I am overwhelmed by how many people graciously shared their experiences, stories and research with me, including many friends, family members, past professors, and colleagues. They are named and recognized throughout the book. One of my favorite parts of this whole process was talking to you and weaving your words and work into the book.

While I was writing, I relied on a couple of close friends and my boys' teachers. Parents have always been important educators in their children's lives, but since COVID-19, their teaching responsibilities have intensified. Because of this, I wanted to write something that would help parents without formal education backgrounds. Christi Adams, thank you for being the "other mother" for my boys, and helping me develop so many of the ideas for this book, before there was a book. Elizabeth Zimmerman and Wake Norris, thank you for your early support and ongoing encouragement. Cara Miller and Tiana Berry-Jones, thank you for brainstorming with me and believing this book could be for parents. And to a magical teacher trio: Lisa Patterson, Emily Lovelace, and Tess Dawson—you are exceptional educators who have become dear friends. Thank you for being there for my boys and for helping make sure this book would be worth your time.

My colleagues in Virginia deserve a special shout-out. I have had the privilege and pleasure of being a part of the *Virginia Is for Learners* movement and launch of the *Commonwealth Learning Partnership*. Through this, I have seen what is possible in our schools when it comes to young people getting ready for a changing world. Of special note, thank you Julie Rautio for helping me figure out how much alliteration is too much alliteration, Gena Keller for being a constant cheerleader for this work, and Leah Dozier Walker for helping me figure out how to be honest and bold when talking about racial justice and equity.

To my past and present colleagues at JFF: you have shaped and sharpened so much of this book. Thank you, Adria Steinberg, Cassius Johnson, and Rebecca Wolfe for early support when I confessed that I wanted to write a book (while working and parenting full-time). Big thanks to Lucretia Murphy for your grounding (and frequent) advice to just write the book, and say what I mean. Thank you, Steve Yadzinski, Nate Anderson, Joe Deegan, Sarah Lamback, Amy Girardi, and Lexie Waugh for helping me think of creative ways to frame the chapters on tomorrow's world and credentials. Thank you, Rachel Crofut and Ichiro Ashihara for sharing your touching personal stories. Thank you, Amy Loyd, for some final review and thinking. And thanks to Julita Bailey-Vasco and Karyl Levinson for being such strong supporters in the background.

Other book and chapter shapers include Julia Freeland Fisher, the original impetus behind this book, and whose influence spreads through my chapter on Connections; as well as Taylor Jo Isenberg, who helped organize the chapter on Cash. Thanks to my past professor, Mark Rank, for an inspiring interview and for letting me adopt the concept of "livable lives."

To my former colleagues at the Forum for Youth Investment and Corporation for a Skilled Workforce: our vision and goals for *The Readiness*

Project and *Connecting Credentials* campaign live on in this book. Special thanks to Caitlin Johnson and Karen Pittman, my incredible co-directors of *The Readiness Project*. All of our thinking and conversations are the cornerstone of *Making It*.

To my former students, co-workers, and partners at Shearwater and Dysart: you have shaped and sharpened so much of my thinking and so many of my beliefs. Thank you for sharing your lives and challenges with me. Your strength, frustrations, and power keep me in this work and keep me pushing for real and lasting change.

Finally, I owe thanks to a few people who may never know this book was written:

David Leeb and Peter Hovmand: as professors of mine first in community college and then graduate school, you each saw in me the spark of a future writer. Thank you for pushing me to get better and learn the rules.

Patrick Boyle: my first editor. Thank you for teaching me the journalist rules of writing. I will always be grateful that you not only edited my work but taught me why you did what you did.

Bill and Sally Canfield: you invested in me when I needed it most. Thank you for the gift of time, reflection, and space to heal after years on the education frontlines. You gave me so much, including our family's first real vacation, and the chance to pause and come up with many of the ideas that are found in these pages.

Finally, Frank. Even though I never found you after I left rehab at 15, you changed my life forever. Thank you for believing that I was more than a dropout and more than a kid with a drinking problem. Your adamant belief that I could and should go to college changed everything for me. Thanks for helping me make it after all.

ABOUT THE AUTHOR

Stephanie Malia Krauss is a mom of two with a background in education, youth development, and social work. Stephanie has been a teacher, coach, school leader, and nonprofit executive. Today she consults with leaders across the United States helping them to design better ways for kids and families to get the education, supports, and experiences they need to make it and thrive. She is a senior advisor at Jobs for the Future and a staff consultant for the Youth Transition Funders Group.

Her website is www.stephaniemaliakrauss.com.

INDEX